CONTENTS

THIS IS PAPER 1

James Carney

FORUM PUBLICATIONS LTD.

Published by
Forum Publications Ltd.
23 Washington Street, Cork
Tel: (021) 4270525 · (021) 4270500
Fax: (01) 6335347

Edited by: Brian Forristal and Billy Ramsell
with the assistance of Claire Maloney

Additional assistance from Edward O'Dwyer

Special thanks to the principal and students of Kinsale Community School, and to Laura Palmer

Design and layout: Dominic Carroll

ISBN: 978-1-906565-05-3

3

Introduction

This is a simple, straightforward book. It is divided into four sections:

- The first section provides basic information and know-how about the exam.
- Section 2 deals with the comprehension question.
- Section 3 deals with the short composition (Q1. B).
- Section 4 deals with long compositions (Q2).

The book teaches you how easy it is to get a good grade in each of the questions on the Paper 1 exam, as long as you follow some simple rules and procedures. It is designed to show that there is nothing mysterious about the way the marks are awarded for this exam. The book shows how marks are won and lost according to strict and definite rules – rules that if you follow will lead you to success.

1 The language styles

There are five language styles: language of information, language of argument, language of persuasion, language of narration and the aesthetic use of language.

INTRODUCTION

The Leaving Cert focuses on five different ways of using language. These are known as the five language styles.

- The language of information, which we use to give information.
- The language of argument, which we use to make an argument.
- The language of persuasion, which we use to persuade people that a particular point of view is correct.
- The language of narration, which we use to tell a story.
- The aesthetic use of language, which involves using language in a way that is artistically pleasing.

Certain genres are associated with certain language styles. For example, reports tend to use the language of information a lot, while adverts tend to use the language of persuasion.

It is important to note, however, that many pieces of writing use more than one language style. For example, a short story might use the language of narration and the aesthetic use of language. A magazine article might mix the language of persuasion and the language of argument.

THE LANGUAGE OF INFORMATION

Not surprisingly, we use the language of information when we want to give the reader information. An informative piece of writing should focus on presenting the relevant information in a clear, concise, objective manner. A good piece of informative writing will emphasise the facts rather than the writer's own opinions.

The following biographical note on the controversial Romantic poet, Lord Byron, is a good example of informative writing.

George Gordon Byron was born on 22 January 1788 and inherited the barony in 1798. He went to school in Dulwich, and then in 1801 to Harrow. In 1805 he went up to Trinity College, Cambridge, later gaining a reputation in London for his startling good looks and extravagant behaviour. His first collection of poems, *Hours of Idleness* (1807), was not well received, but with the publication of the first two cantos of *Childe Harold's Pilgrimage* (1812) he became famous overnight, and increased his fame with a series of wildly popular 'Eastern Tales'. In 1815 he married the heiress Annabella Milbanke, but they were separated after a year. Byron shocked society by the rumoured relationship with his half-sister, Augusta, and in 1816 he left England forever. He settled eventually in Italy, where he lived for some time with Teresa, Countess Guiccioli. He supported Italian revolutionary movements, and in 1823 left for Greece to fight in its struggle for independence, but he contracted a fever and died at Missolonghi in 1824.

This notice satisfies all the basic criteria for a good piece of informative writing:

- It is **economical**. Despite the fact that there are many book-length biographies of Byron, this short sample of writing still manages to convey all the important details of his life in a single paragraph.

- It is **straightforward**. There is nothing in the piece that is likely to confuse the reader or leave them questioning what it means.

- It is **objective**. Although Byron was a very controversial figure, the piece does not judge either his actions or his work. You will notice, for example, that it does not state that he did or did not have a relationship with his half-sister, only that it was *rumoured* that he did. Similarly, it does not comment on the intrinsic merit of Byron's poetry; it just notes whether it was received well or badly. The same features are evident in the following two examples of informative writing, both published on Wikipedia. The first is an entry for the moon; the second provides instructions on how to make an omelette.

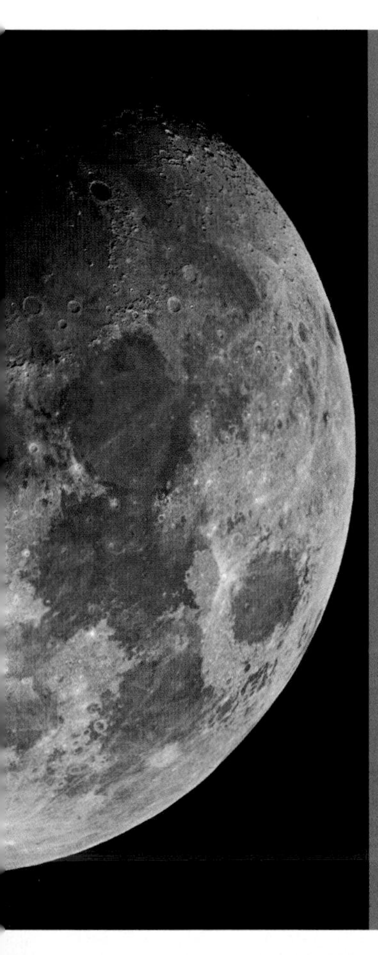

The Moon

The Moon (Latin: *Luna*) is Earth's only natural satellite and the fifth largest natural satellite in the Solar System. The average centre-to-centre distance from the Earth to the Moon is 384,403 km, about thirty times the diameter of the Earth. The Moon's diameter is 3,474 km, a little more than a quarter that of the Earth. This means that the Moon's volume is about 2 per cent that of Earth and the pull of gravity at its surface about 17 per cent that of the Earth. The Moon makes a complete orbit around the Earth every 27.3 days, and the periodic variations in the geometry of the Earth–Moon–Sun system are responsible for the lunar phases that repeat every 29.5 days.

The Moon is the only celestial body to which humans have travelled and upon which humans have landed. The first artificial object to escape Earth's gravity and pass near the Moon was the Soviet Union's Luna 1, the first artificial object to impact the lunar surface was Luna 2, and the first photographs of the normally occluded far side of the Moon were made by Luna 3, all in 1959. The first spacecraft to perform a successful lunar soft landing was Luna 9, and the first unmanned vehicle to orbit the Moon was Luna 10, both in 1966. The United States' (U.S.) Apollo programme achieved the only manned missions to date, resulting in six landings between 1969 and 1972. Human exploration of the Moon ceased with the conclusion of the Apollo programme, although several countries have announced plans to send people or robotic spacecraft to the Moon.

How to make an omelette

You will only be using one egg yoke and three egg whites, so the first thing you need to do is separate two of the yokes from the eggs. You can use a tool for this step or just crack the egg open and use your hand to 'catch' the yoke and let the white go into the bowl (removing the two egg yokes, you will cut the fat from the omelette and the taste will not be effected). Beat your eggs until they are nice and frothy; then set aside. Slice your bell pepper in half, remove the seeds, slice some strips of bell pepper, dice the strips, put the diced bell pepper into a bowl. Dice the onion – use as much or little as you want. Put the diced onion into the bowl with the bell pepper; then set aside. Core the tomato and remove the seeds by gently squeezing the tomato (do this over a sink or have a bowl below the tomato to catch the seeds and juice). Dice the tomato, and place the tomato in its own bowl; then set aside. Slice the bacon into small pieces, and place in a bowl; then set aside. Place a small amount of cheese into a bowl; then set aside. Get your spinach ready by placing it in a bowl.

Now we are going to start the cooking process. First we are going to get our filling ready. Turn on a burner to medium heat, place the pan on the burner, and lightly spray with olive oil. Add the diced bell peppers and onions to the pan. Sauté until the onion softs up (about 3 to 5 minutes). Add the bacon pieces to the pan, and sauté until the bacon is cooked. Add the spinach – make sure you use a pretty good amount of spinach as it will cook down to almost nothing (this process takes about 3 minutes or so. Place your filling into a bowl and set aside …

THE LANGUAGE OF ARGUMENT

The language of argument is used when a writer wants to convince us that some particular point of view is true. A good piece of argumentative writing will appeal to the reader's power of reasoning. It will not rely upon emotion, hearsay or personal experience, but will attempt to make claims that *anyone*, regardless of their personal background or experience, will recognise as being true.

Consider this article from the *Financial Times*, which looks to convince us of the merits of nuclear power. There are several reasons why this is a good piece of argumentative writing. The writer makes a point and then backs it up by reference to facts and statistics. He tries to convince us that he is right by arranging these facts into a logical, coherent argument. He avoids emotive language and 'real life' examples that tug on our heartstrings. The writer appeals to our heads, not to our hearts.

Financial Times, September 20, 2006
Michael Backman

IS URANIUM a good bet? If the evidence from Asia is anything to go by, the answer is yes. The economies of China and India are growing fast. Neither produce enough power for existing requirements.

The US government's National Intelligence Council has estimated that India's energy consumption will at least double by 2020. China's will rise by 150 per cent. That heralds an environmental disaster.

Why? Because the power that both produce comes largely from the dirtiest, most harmful means: burning coal. The situation is unsustainable. Nuclear power is an obvious solution and, in a few decades, Asia could be home to at least half the world's nuclear reactors.

Coal burning accounts for about 70 per cent of the energy produced in China, compared with a global average of about 25 per cent. China wants to get this down to 60 per cent by 2020, but even if it is possible, it will mean coal-generated power will dramatically increase in absolute terms.

As things stand, China uses more coal than the US, the European Union and Japan combined, and its coal consumption this year is up 14 per cent on last year. According to one report, a new coal-fired power station opens in China every seven to ten days.

Not surprisingly, China has quickly become one of the most polluted countries. Air quality is abysmal. Official estimates are that 400,000 Chinese die each year from diseases related to air pollution. Separately, the World Bank says sixteen of the world's twenty most polluted cities are in China.

Pollution levels in India are also rising, but the problem is not as acute as in China. Nonetheless, India is stepping up its construction of coal-fired plants, meaning that its greenhouse gas emissions will accelerate. And given that India's population is expected to pass China's in 2030, that's a worrying trend.

Both are looking to generate more power from gas and hydro-electric schemes. But both sources will only slow the rate of growth of greenhouse-gas emissions. And so nuclear energy is looking increasingly viable, and even desirable.

According to the World Nuclear Association, of the 442 operational reactors in the world, almost a quarter, or 109, are in Asia. Another twenty-eight are under construction worldwide. Fifteen of these are in Asia. More are planned, so that in total, 285 nuclear reactors are either operational, under construction, planned or proposed for South and East Asia.

The most nuclear of Asia's economies are South Korea, Japan and Taiwan, which generate forty-five, twenty-nine and twenty per cent respectively of their power from nuclear sources. China's nuclear power plants generate just two per cent and India's 2.8 per cent. This is when, worldwide, nuclear accounts for sixteen per cent of all the power generated. There is room for growth.

THE LANGUAGE OF PERSUASION

We use the language of persuasion when we want to persuade someone that a certain point of view is correct. Whereas the language of argument appeals to a person's reason, the language of persuasion appeals to his or her emotions. In this regard, it is important to realise that the language of persuasion is a lot 'dirtier' than the language of argument: unlike logical argumentation, where an argument will stand or fall by its own merits, the language of persuasion will often appeal to personal prejudices and beliefs that have no real bearing on the truth of the claims being made.

The following article, taken from the UK edition of *The Sun* newspaper (6 January 2007), is a good example of persuasive writing. In it, the writer attempts to persuade the reader that the European Human Rights Act undermines British independence in combating crime.

THE Sun

FREE PICTURE TO YOUR MOBILE

EXCLUSIVE INTERVIEW

I still can't believe it... now for No1

I'll take my mum on her first hol

SHAYNE

KERRY: YOU ARE DEAD

Star's bust-up at airport

Saddam speaks to The Sun

THE Sun

FREE DVD

No1 FOOTBALL PULLOUT INSIDE

NATIONWIDE HUNT

JOHN REID'S BRAIN IS MISSING

Fears for Home Sec over full jails fiasco

Chaos in snow sprinkle

Guards' African officer

THE Sun

BIGGEST TICKET GIVEAWAY EVER

YOU BLUE IT

Chelsea miss chance to close on Man Utd

ROYAL EXCLUSIVE

QUEEN: I SUPPORT ARSENAL

Gooner like her mother

GMTV phone 'rip-off'

WRONG RIGHTS

IT is a law that puts the interests of the guilty above those of the innocent.

It protects terrorists rather than the lives of people they want to blow to smithereens.

It creates an atmosphere where a murder suspect can skip the country with his face hidden by a Muslim woman's veil.

Welcome to the crazy world of the Human Rights Act, quoted by idiots at Derbyshire Police as one reason they refused to release photographs of two vicious murderers who escaped from jail TWO MONTHS ago!

Once the stupidity of this excuse was exposed, there was a crashing sound as Government ministers and cops went into reverse gear.

It beggars belief that police — paid to protect the public — can become so foolishly obsessed with political correctness that they arrogantly put the 'human rights' of murderers before doing their duty.

This Government reckons that the 1998 law and the signing of the European Human Rights Convention is one of its proudest achievements.

In fact, letting British laws be determined by unelected judges and a ludicrous court in Strasbourg is an insult to our democracy.

Restoring common sense to our justice system is one of the great challenges facing Gordon Brown when he takes over in Downing Street.

THE Sun

QE2 IS SET TO SAIL FOR WAR

We told you first

GOTCHA

Our lads sink gunboat and hole cruiser

SUNK

CRIPPLED

BATTLE FOR THE ISLANDS

UNION BOYCOTTS WAR

£50,000 BINGO! Today's lucky numbers are on Page 20

The article demonstrates many features commonly associated with the language of persuasion as it is used in opinion pieces:

- It does not rely on any form of rigorous or balanced argumentation for its persuasive force
- It is written in strong language that appeals to the emotions. Words such as 'crazy', 'arrogantly' and 'insult' are designed to provoke anger and disbelief in the reader.
- It makes references to facts 'everybody' knows to be true, without making any attempt to prove that these facts are correct.
- It uses **bold type** and CAPITAL LETTERS to emphasise an important point, and it certainly doesn't leave out the exclamation marks!!! (This is a common feature of opinion pieces in tabloid newspapers like *The Sun* and *The Star*).

All of this manipulation is quite conscious, and there's a good chance the editor doesn't even believe what he's written himself. Don't be the dupe that falls for it.

THE LANGUAGE OF NARRATION

We use the language of narration when we want to tell a story (a story can also be referred to as a narrative). Narratives can be fictional, factual or a mixture of the two. The language of narration is concerned with actions, characters and events.

The following extract from *The Fourth Crusade* by Jonathan Philips provides us with a good example of factual narrative writing. A mixture of foreign forces called the Fourth Crusade has sailed across the channel and is attempting to scale the walls of Constantinople:

The walls of the Blachernae Palace did not come down to the shore and the Crusaders disembarked from their ships and concentrated their attack on the narrow strip of land between the fortifications and the water. Both sides launched a deadly bombardment of rocks and missiles. The first men ashore unloaded ladders and other fighting equipment under heavy enemy fire. As the Crusaders heaved their wooden burden towards the walls, the first arrows thudded into shields and armour. They rarely pierced the chain mail and its protective padding right through to the flesh (or if they did, caused only a light wound), yet the arrows stayed fixed to their prey and the soldiers began to resemble giant porcupines covered with feathered quills. As they started to mount the walls, the two forces meshed together and the exchange of missiles was supplemented by the thrust of lances and the swing of axes and swords. Some of those on the scaling ladders were pushed away from the walls to fall backwards in a deadly, graceful arc; others were prised from their ladders and plummeted to the ground to die or sustain crippling injuries; still more were killed by sword blows as they climbed. The cries of the injured and dying, of orders bellowed in Greek, Danish, Italian, German and French, the occasional blast from the imperial trumpeters, and the crashing and splintering of missiles exploding into fragments against the city walls comprised a truly hellish cacophony.

This extract from Jane Austen's *Pride and Prejudice* is a good example of fictional narrative writing:

Elizabeth, as they drove along, watched for the first appearance of Pemberley Woods with some perturbation; and when at length they turned in at the lodge, her spirits were in a high flutter.

The park was very large, and contained great variety of ground. They entered it in one of its lowest points, and drove for some time through a beautiful wood, stretching over a wide extent.

Elizabeth's mind was too full for conversation, but she saw and admired every remarkable spot and point of view. They gradually ascended for half a mile, and then found themselves at the top of a considerable eminence, where the wood ceased, and the eye was instantly caught by Pemberley House, situated on the opposite side of a valley, into which the road with some abruptness wound.

These are well-written pieces of narrative writing, but it is important to remember that the language of narration does not just feature in novels, short stories and history books. We use it all the time in everyday life: when we tell jokes, share a piece of gossip or describe a night out to a friend.

THE AESTHETIC USE OF LANGUAGE

We can also use language in a way that is creative and original. We can attempt to bring out the strangeness and beauty of words, and create something that is artistically pleasing. This is known as the aesthetic use of language. We often associate the aesthetic use of language with short stories, but it can also occur in non-fiction writing. The following are just a few of the ways in which language can be used aesthetically.

RHYTHM Sometimes writing can create an artistically pleasing effect through the rhythm of its words. We see this at the end of James Joyce's short story, *The Dead*, which is famous for its rhythmic, hypnotic effect:

A few light taps upon the pane made him turn to the window. It had begun to snow again. He watched sleepily the flakes, silver and dark, falling obliquely against the lamplight. The time had come for him to set out on his journey westward. Yes, the newspapers were right: snow was general all over Ireland. It was falling on every part of the dark central plain, on the treeless hills, falling softly upon the Bog of Allen and, farther westward, softly falling into the dark mutinous Shannon waves. It was falling, too, upon every part of the lonely churchyard on the hill where Michael Furey lay buried. It lay thickly drifted on the crooked crosses and headstones, on the spears of the little gate, on the barren thorns. His soul swooned slowly as he heard the snow falling faintly through the universe and faintly falling, like the descent of their last end, upon all the living and the dead.

REPETITION The careful use of repetition can give a piece of writing a power and artistically pleasing effect. We see this in Martin Luther King's famous 'I have a dream' speech:

I have a dream that one day even the state of Mississippi, a state sweltering with the heat of injustice, sweltering with the heat of oppression, will be transformed into an oasis of freedom and justice.

I have a dream that my four little children will one day live in a nation where they will not be judged by the colour of their skin but by the content of their character.

I have a *dream* today!

It is also evident in the opening passage of Charles Dickens' *A Tale of Two Cities*:

> **It was the best of times, it was the worst of times, it was the age of wisdom, it was the age of foolishness, it was the epoch of belief, it was the epoch of incredulity, it was the season of Light, it was the season of Darkness, it was the spring of hope, it was the winter of despair, we had everything before us, we had nothing before us, we were all going direct to Heaven, we were all going direct the other way – in short, the period was so far like the present period, that some of its noisiest authorities insisted on its being received, for good or for evil, in the superlative degree of comparison only.**

METAPHORS AND SIMILES

An aesthetically pleasing effect can also be created through the inventive use of metaphor and simile. The use of a good metaphor or simile can bring something vividly to life in the mind of the reader. In *London Fields*, for example, Martin Amis compares the plumes of cigarette smoke in a snooker club to the ghosts of referees. In *The Big Sleep*, Raymond Chandler describes a balding man as follows: 'A few locks of dry white hair clung to his scalp, like wild flowers fighting for life on a bare rock'.

EUPHONY AND CACOPHONY

Euphony occurs when a sentence or passage has a pleasant or musical sound, often created by a combination of similar vowel sounds and the use of soft consonants.

Cacophony occurs when a sentence or passage has an unpleasant, jarring or harsh sound, often created by the use of hard consonants.

IMAGERY

Writers can also create a pleasing, aesthetic effect by describing something in a fresh, vivid and original way.

2 How to get the marks

This is a guide to how marks are won and lost in the marking of Leaving Cert compositions. It refers to short compositions (Section 1B) and long compositions (Section 2). Short-story writing is something of a 'special case', and will be addressed separately.

30% PURPOSE

It is vital your composition fulfils the purpose for which it was intended. The Leaving Cert examiners refer to this as 'Clarity of Purpose'. Thirty per cent of all marks in every single question are awarded for this.

If you keep your wits about you, it is relatively easy to score well in this section of the marking scheme. But you also need to recognise that it's very much an all-or-nothing affair: if you misread the question, for example, and write a stunning essay that is completely beside the point, it is in this section that you will be penalised. The lesson? Always read the question carefully. Let me repeat that: Always read the question carefully.

BE RELEVANT Your composition must be relevant to the question or essay title. Therefore, you must always read the question carefully. I really can't stress this enough.

REMAIN FOCUSED FROM BEGINNING TO END Your composition must be focused. It is no good to start writing in response to the question or essay title if, by the halfway stage, you have drifted off the topic completely. Every single paragraph must be relevant.

HAVE A CLEAR AIM OR POINT OF VIEW Your composition must have a clear aim. It is almost always best to state the goal or objective of your composition in the first or second paragraph. Everything in the composition must serve this aim.

Some questions require you to argue for a point of view. Some don't. However, it is often best to adopt a point of view anyway. This will help your essay to have a clear aim. You can state your point of view in the first or second paragraph, and use the rest of the essay to support this point of view. For instance, if you are asked to write about social-networking sites, decide whether you are for or against them, and use the language of persuasion and argument to try to persuade your readers that your point of view is correct.

BE CONSCIOUS OF GENRE

Have you been asked to write in a specific genre – for example a letter or a speech? If so, you must reproduce what are known as the 'conventions of the genre'. A letter must feature the address of the person you are writing to, and a speech should begin with a salutation (for example, 'Ladies and gentlemen').

30% COHERENCE

It is vital that your composition holds together as a coherent and well-organised piece of writing. The Leaving Cert examiners refer to this as 'Coherency of Delivery'. Thirty per cent of all marks are awarded for this.

CONTROL YOUR TONE AND REGISTER

Be conscious of the tone in which you are writing. Are you writing in a formal, semi-formal or a light-hearted tone? It is usually best to maintain the same tone throughout. If you slip from a formal to an informal tone halfway through your composition, you will lose marks unless it is for a very, very good reason.

MANAGE YOUR IDEAS, REFERENCES AND EXAMPLES

In your composition, you will probably deal with a number of topics, introducing various ideas, references and examples. Always ensure that they are a hundred per cent relevant to your aim. Furthermore, don't let them sidetrack you. If you mention Live Aid in a composition on charity, don't start writing about Bob Geldof's love life. Just make the relevant point about Live Aid and then move on to your next topic.

SEQUENCE YOUR TOPICS CAREFULLY

Your composition will make several different points and introduce different topics. It is important that these are arranged in a coherent order: a sequence that makes the composition easy to read and allows it to fulfil its aim. Two things are important here: planning and practise. Before you start writing your essay, think this through carefully. Sketch out several different sequences and decide on which one works best. This is time well spent. The more you practise, the easier this will become.

30% LANGUAGE USE

This aspect of the marking scheme deals with how well you use and manipulate language. Thirty per cent of all marks are awarded for this.

VARY YOUR VOCABULARY

Displaying a large and varied vocabulary in the Leaving Cert testifies to your ability to manipulate language, and it is advisable to vary your vocabulary in order to avoid repetition. However, always use vocabulary that serves the aim of your composition. For example, if you are writing a short talk for foreign students, you will want to avoid long, complicated and unusual words. Never use a word unless you know what it means and how to use it properly.

USE LIVELY AND INTERESTING PHRASING

You will be rewarded for using language in a lively and interesting way, so if you have a flair for language, let the examiner see it. However, always be conscious of the genre in which you are writing. Flowery and poetic language, for instance, might be fine in a personal essay, but might be out of place in an article for a serious journal.

IN GENERAL KEEP YOUR SENTENCES SHORT

Again and again, students use long, over-complicated sentences that confuse the reader. Long sentences also lead to 'errors of syntax': the sentence's words are arranged in the wrong order. In general, it is best keep your sentences short. The longer your sentences are, the more likely you are to confuse both yourself and the reader. This is not to say you should never use long sentences – sometimes they can't be avoided – but try to use them sparingly. As the old mantra goes: the more full stops you have, the less mistakes you make.

VARY YOUR SENTENCE PATTERNS

It is vital that your sentences are not all of the same type. Repetitious sentence patterns will turn the reader off. An example of 'bad' sentence patterning occurs in the following passage:

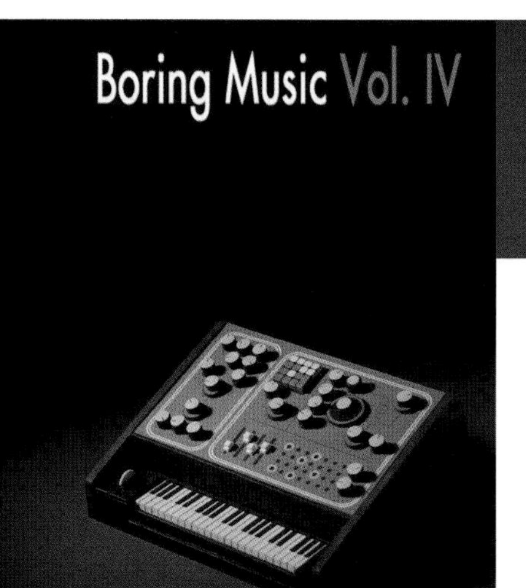

I went to town on the bus. After that I went to Virgin and checked out some new CDs. Then I went to a café and had a sandwich. I met my friends after that. We went to the park and hung around for the afternoon. I went home at six o'clock.

As you can see, most of the sentences in this passage are constructed in the same way: they almost all start off with a personal pronoun and a verb (I went, I met, we went), and subsequently fill in the details. From a grammatical point of view, there is nothing wrong with this; but it makes for a reading experience that is as dull as porridge, and will turn the reader off completely.

To avoid this, you need to vary your sentence construction in such a way that the reader doesn't feel they are reading the same sentence over and over again. Here's an example of how you might do this with the above passage:

I went to town on the bus. As I wouldn't be meeting my friends for a while, I thought I'd take a look at some CDs in Virgin while I was still on my own. Once I'd finished there, I still had some time to spare, so I spent an hour in the café on Connolly Street that I always go to. They do nice sandwiches, so I ordered a tuna melt and spent an hour reading a magazine I'd bought. I met the lads later, but they were broke, so we spent the rest of the afternoon hanging around the park. I made for home at six o'clock, the time of the last bus.

To be fair, the above passage is hardly Pulitzer Prize-winning material, but it does at least vary the sentence patterns that it uses. The net result is a passage that is a lot more engaging for the reader.

USE PARAGRAPHS AND PUNCTUATION PROPERLY

Paragraphs are discussed in the following chapter. A comprehensive section on punctuation can be found at the back of this book.

10% MECHANICS

Ten per cent of the marks are awarded for spelling and grammar, which is known as 'Accuracy of Mechanics'. There is nothing for you to do except learn to spell and use grammar in the right way. This means learning how to spell new words as you encounter them, and familiarising yourself with the rules of grammar.

FRESHNESS, ENERGY & ORIGINALITY

We often associate originality and freshness with short stories, but it is also possible to have these qualities in a non-fiction composition. For instance, you can have a fresh and original take on the topic you are writing about. You can be original by using language in a lively and artistically pleasing manner.

There is room for this kind of thing in many genres – for example, speeches, articles, personal essays and even advertisements. Reports and formal letters probably offer less scope for such originality.

However, before you try to dazzle the examiner with your freshness and originality, make sure you have got the basics right.

FURTHER ADVICE: SHORT STORIES

30% PURPOSE

FOCUS AND RELEVANCE

A short story offers greater freedom than other genres, yet your story must be clearly related to the title you have been given. If it is not, you will lose a lot of marks.

ORIGINALITY AND FRESHNESS

The short story rewards originality and freshness more than any other genre. Your story doesn't need to be crazy or experimental, but you want to avoid being dreary, predictable and obvious. Intriguing characters, a vivid setting and an engrossing plot are all ways of achieving this.

30% COHERENCY

SEQUENCING AND NARRATIVE SHAPE

Your story should be well structured with a defined beginning, middle and end. If your story meanders pointlessly you will lose marks. This is called having a good narrative shape. As we shall see in the chapter on the short story, it is permissible to play with the sequence of your story. For instance, you can begin by telling the final events of the story and then recount the rest as a flashback. However, the events must always make sense to the reader. If you lose the reader, you will also lose marks.

CREATIVE MODELLING You must give a snapshot of the world in which the story happens. The better you are at creating believable characters and vivid settings, the more marks you will get.

CONTROL OF TONE AND REGISTER Sometimes in a story, you will write in voice that is not your own. For example, your narrator might be an old woman or a child. It is important that you maintain this tone or register throughout the entire story. If you lapse out of it, you will lose marks.

30% EFFICIENCY OF LANGUAGE USE

The advice for non-fiction pieces holds true here, but there is an added emphasis on creative modelling – how well you use language to create vivid settings and believable characters.

10% MECHANICS

The advice for non-fiction pieces holds true here. Sometimes in a short story, it may be permissible to deviate from the normal rules of spelling, grammar and syntax – for example, if you are writing in the voice of an uneducated person or if you are writing everyday dialogue. However, only ever do this if you have a very, very good reason, or you will lose marks.

7 GOLDEN RULES OF NON-FICTION COMPOSITION

1. **Make sure every single thing in your composition is relevant to the title.**
2. **Have a clear aim, and state it explicitly in the first or second paragraph.**
3. **Determine which tone (formal or informal) is appropriate, and maintain it throughout.**
4. **One Topic = One Paragraph (see next chapter).**
5. **Sequence your paragraphs in a logical and readable order.**
6. **Introduce relevant references and examples, but don't let them sidetrack you.**
7. **Keep your sentences short, and vary their patterns.**

AND ALWAYS BE AWARE OF THE GENRE IN WHICH YOU ARE WRITING

3 Paragraphs

If you wish to do well in the Leaving Cert essay, it is essential that you master the basics of how to organise your work into paragraphs. The present chapter will provide you with an overview of proper paragraphing. As an added plus, this information will also be of use to you when writing answers in Paper 2, where you will also need to display an awareness of how to use paragraphs.

PARAGRAPH STRUCTURE

WHAT IS A PARAGRAPH?

Essentially, a paragraph is a collection of one or more sentences that relate to the same idea. Because essays seek to relate ideas together in a coherent discussion, this means that paragraphs can be considered one of the basic units of composition.

When writing essays in the Leaving Cert, it is vitally important that you master the skill of properly arranging your work into paragraphs. A good insight into paragraph structure will force you to articulate your thoughts in a clear and effective way. The following are the hallmarks of a well-structured paragraph:

- The first line of each paragraph is normally indented. Alternatively, a line is skipped to indicate the start of a new paragraph.
- The subject or topic of a paragraph is often stated in the first sentence, which is called a 'topic' sentence.
- The remaining sentences develop the topic sentences and are known as 'body' sentences.
- The paragraph is unified, with all the sentences contributing to create a single idea.
- A paragraph is complete when the idea the writer wants to express is brought clearly into focus.

PARAGRAPH LENGTH

Be sure that your paragraphs are concerned with *only one* idea or event. The whole purpose of paragraphs is to make it easy for the reader to see how the different issues you discuss relate to one another, and this is only possible if each paragraph communicates only one idea or action.

The length of the paragraph is determined by the importance of the idea or action you are describing. There is no 'correct' length for a paragraph. Some paragraphs can be very long, while others may only last for a single sentence. On the whole, try to avoid consistently writing paragraphs that are either too long or too short. A collection of short paragraphs looks unstructured and is irritating to read, while a series of over-long paragraphs makes it difficult to determine the relationship between the ideas that are being discussed.

STARTING A NEW PARAGRAPH

Paragraphs should be distinguished from each other in one of two ways (but never both in the same essay): either the first line of a new paragraph is indented, or a line is skipped. When skipping lines, always skip from the line containing the last word of the previous paragraph, even if this line contains only one world.

The paragraph structure of your essay should conform to one of these two forms:

INDENTED PARAGRAPHS

It had happened at last. The expected message had come. All his life, it seemed to him, he had been waiting for this to happen.

He was walking down the long corridor at the Ministry and he was almost at the spot where Julia had slipped the note into his hand when he became aware that someone larger than himself was walking just behind him. The person, whoever it was, gave a small cough, evidently as a prelude to speaking. Winston stopped abruptly and turned. It was O'Brien.

At last they were face to face, and it seemed that his only impulse was to run away. His heart bounded violently. He would have been incapable of speaking. O'Brien, however, had continued forward in the same movement, laying a friendly hand for a moment on Winston's arm, so that the two of them were walk-ing side by side. He began speaking with the peculiar grave courtesy that differentiated him from the majority of Inner Party members.

SKIPPED-LINE PARAGRAPHS

It had happened at last. The expected message had come. All his life, it seemed to him, he had been waiting for this to happen.

He was walking down the long corridor at the Ministry and he was almost at the spot where Julia had slipped the note into his hand, when he became aware that someone larger than himself was walking just behind him. The person, whoever it was, gave a small cough, evidently as a prelude to speaking. Winston stopped abruptly and turned. It was O'Brien.

At last they were face to face, and it seemed that his only impulse was to run away. His heart bounded violently. He would have been incapable of speaking. O'Brien, however, had continued forward in the same movement, laying a friendly hand for a moment on Winston's arm, so that the two of them were walking side by side. He began speaking with the peculiar grave courtesy that differentiated him from the majority of Inner Party members.

Whichever of these paragraph styles you use is entirely up to yourself, but it is important that you are consistent. If you start using an indented style, use the indented style throughout your essay, and the same applies for the skipped-line style.

TOPIC SENTENCES

We call the first sentence of a paragraph a 'topic' sentence. This should tell the reader what the paragraph is going to be about. In order to come up with an effective topic sentence, you must be clear in your own mind what you want the paragraph to be about.

Topic sentences should also relate the topic you introduce to topics that have been explored in previous paragraphs. An essay is not just a collection of isolated points, but a sustained discussion that links these points together. Consequently, it is important that a topic sentence clearly states the link between the new idea and the paragraph that went before it.

BODY SENTENCES

After the topic sentence, the remainder of a paragraph consists of what are known as 'body' sentences. The central purpose of these sentences is to develop the idea introduced by the topic sentence.

Your central goal when writing a paragraph is to ensure that all your body sentences relate to the idea articulated by the topic sentence. This simply means not drifting off the topic and introducing irrelevant material.

IMPORTANT NOTE

Before moving on, it is worth giving just one final word about paragraphs. Although the advice on paragraph structure given above is sound, and you should make every effort to follow it, you will not have to look far to find examples of published writing that seem to contradict it. Do not take this to mean that it is okay for you to do the same. The rules of composition are not absolute, and there will always be good writers who ignore the conventions. These writers, however, are masters of their trade, and if they ignore the rules, it is only because they've already proved they can follow them. You have yet to prove this, so until a Nobel Prize for Literature comes your way, you're best advised to stay within the rules of the game.

4 Planning your writing

In the Leaving Cert, it is vital that you plan before you write. (This advice applies to both long and short compositions: Section 1B and Section 2.)

HOW TO PLAN YOUR COMPOSITION

When planning, you should take the following steps:

READ THE QUESTION CAREFULLY Understand what you are being asked to do.

BRAINSTORM Free your mind and write down everything that comes into your head associated with the topic, no matter how silly it seems. At this stage, the more ideas you have, the better.

SELECT WHICH IDEAS YOU ARE GOING TO USE Base your decision on freshness, originality and, above all, relevance. Check again to make sure that every idea you are going to discuss is relevant to the question.

SEQUENCE YOUR PARAGRAPHS By now, you should have a list of ideas or topics that you are going to include in your essay. Each idea is going to have one paragraph devoted to it. You must decide in which order these paragraphs are going to appear. Your goal is to find the order that is most logical and readable. If you have time, play around with different sequences in order to find the one that will work best.

PLANNING YOUR ANSWERS TO THE COMPREHENSION QUESTIONS You should always read the question carefully. You don't need an elaborate plan, but you should quickly jot down the main points you want to make, and think about the order in which they should appear. This will guide you as you write and prevent you wandering off the point.

5 Comprehension

Comprehension (*noun*): understanding, grasp, conception, apprehension, cognition, ken, knowledge, awareness, perception, interpretation.
***Antonym*: ignorance.**

INTRODUCTION

The following is a good way to approach the comprehension questions:

- Once you have decided which text you are going to answer on, read it from start to finish.
- Carefully read the questions.
- Read the text again with the questions in mind, underlining passages that are relevant to the questions you are being asked.
- Quickly read through the text for a third time.
- Briefly plan your first answer, jotting down the main points you want to make. Think about the order in which points should appear. This will guide you as you write, and prevent you wandering off the point.
- Remember to quote from, and refer to, the text at all times in order to support the points you want to make.

SAMPLE ANSWER 1

It takes more than wizardry to nurture reading

David Milofsky

You can't blame parents, librarians and educators for hoping that the remarkable popularity of J.K. Rowling's Harry Potter books would translate into a renaissance for young readers. Booksellers, too, were eager to jump onto the bandwagon and market a variety of Young Adult titles to the newly literate.

Unfortunately, studies have indicated that despite Harry Potter, young people aren't reading any more than they used to. In fact, the rate of books read may have gone down. While the hope had been that the frenzy brought on by the series demonstrated that kids really do like to read, the truth turns out to be somewhat different: kids like to read Harry Potter – otherwise, they'd rather play video games.

The findings of such studies are sobering indeed for those of us who value books and reading. Sunil Iyengar, director of research and analysis behind one of the studies, says that 'Young people across the board, not just teenagers, but younger adults between 18 and 34, are reading much less than they used to. And we're not just talking about rates of leisure reading, but the actual ability to read.'

This isn't too surprising to some of us, but the cause for worry at these conclusions may go beyond the obvious. Iyengar went on: 'Researchers have found that there's a strong correlation between reading and success in school, employment decisions, job satisfaction and even volunteer work in civic organisations.' So, in other words, readers are more likely not only to be better students, which one might expect, but also more employable and better citizens. Thus, improving reading rates is in the best interests not only of a handful of scruffy authors, but also of business and civic leaders.

From Potter to Dickens? Is there hope?

The only good news here is the fact that reading rates among teenagers and young adults, if falling, must be falling from somewhere. According to Iyengar, children up to age 13 are generally good and enthusiastic readers. Why is a mystery, but something seems to happen in early adolescence and young adulthood that turns people away from reading as a leisure activity. If this development could somehow be turned around, the theory goes, the downward trend might be reversed, and the love of reading be re-instilled in teenagers and young people.

And so we are brought back to the Harry Potter phenomenon. Books, like everything else in modern society, must endure styles and fads, temporary enthusiasms that fade over time. Think Jacqueline Susann, Harold Robbins or Grace Metalius. Publishers, like other businesses, introduce and advertise books hoping to build familiarity and loyalty, and thus 'brand-name' authors.

continued over

continued from previous page

Despite the treacle of Rowling's prose, her Potter tomes have obviously struck a nerve, and not only with adolescent readers. Adults and college students were also up at midnight waiting in line for the latest installment of the series, and talking excitedly about coded references to *Beowulf* and other classics. Whatever one might think of Rowling's novels, you never hear Updike or Roth discussed with such fervour around a dinner table or the water cooler.

The difference between this phenomenon and days of yore is not, I'm quick to add, one of quality. Those of us who discovered reading through the *Hardy Boys* mysteries or *Nancy Drew* can hardly claim higher moral ground than Potter enthusiasts. But the way of the past was that, having been drawn in by these formulaic stories, young readers would eventually move on to more serious literature, and, in so doing, make reading a lifelong entertainment.

Whether this ever happened in large numbers is open to question. What is clear, though, is that it's not happening anymore. After finishing a Harry Potter mystery, your average young reader is much more likely to move over to the computer to check out YouTube or MySpace than to head to the library in search of something by Joseph Conrad or Charles Dickens. More's the pity, but that's the contemporary reality against which we must now just hope.

QUESTIONS

(i) 'The findings of such studies are sobering indeed': What does the writer find 'sobering' or disturbing about the findings of studies into younger people's reading habits? **10**

(ii) What differences does the writer establish between reading habits of the past and those of today? **10**

(iii) Did you find the argument put forward in this article convincing? Support your view with reference to the text. **20**

ANSWERS

(i) From this passage the writer has uncovered statistics that suggest the 'rate of books read' has decreased in recent years, despite the remarkable success of J.K. Rowling's 'Harry Potter' books. Experts had thought that the amount of people, young and old, who read books would increase because of books such as Harry Potter. Researchers find these statistics 'sobering' as they would like to see the value of books and reading survive instead of being lost in a modern world of video games, Internet and television.

(ii) The writer highlights key facts about the difference between reading habits of the past and present. The author states that the reading 'phenomenon' of today is not one of quality and that once kids are finished with the Harry Potter 'phase' they will forget about reading and go back to their favourite pastime of television or video games. The point he is making is that those people who grew up reading books like 'Nancy Drew' etc, had eventually moved up the ladder to 'serious literature'. It is hoped that eventually, Potter fans might follow in their footsteps.

COMMENTARY

Badly written.

The student has been asked about the writer's attitude to the topic but her answer focuses more on researchers and experts quoted in the piece and on the success of Harry Potter books. Her answer neglects to mention the writer's belief that reading produces better citizens and employees. The answer also contains some poor writing. **3/10**

The student addresses the key point here: that in the past, light reading encouraged children to develop a taste for literature, whereas in the present, this doesn't seem to be happening. While the student quotes from, and makes reference to, the piece, the answer could be better written and more clearly constructed. **7/10**

(iii) I find this piece convincing yes, but do not agree with it myself. I have grown up reading the Harry Potter books and now that the saga is finished, find it hard to find a book that lives up to the same standard as J.K's brilliant books. This might explain the down trend in the rate of people who read books but I am sure, before long some other author, such as the up and coming Darren Shan, will capture the attention of the lost Potter audience and captivate them enough to get the rate of reading to increase again.

This sentence is long and awkward, and might be better broken into shorter, clearer sentences.

The amount of people reading, really depends on the right book being published in the right time, with a popular theme or issue of the age being portrayed in it. So, yes there is still hope for the value of books and reading surviving this modern age, despite the statistics. Expecting the Harry Potter generation to move onto Dickens is unrealistic as its language and themes are not the same as today. So give to time and kids might once again abandon the 'video games' or 'you tube' to be involved in the next book 'phenomenon'.

The student's answer is confusing. She says that she finds the writer's argument convincing but then claims to disagree with him on almost every point. The student should have outlined what elements of the writer's argument she found convincing before coming in with her own reservations about his overall point. As it stands, she focuses more on her own point of view than on the author's argument. **12/30**

Total mark: 22/50 (D3)

Beating the Bebo addiction

The social networking website Bebo has just celebrated its first birthday. Already it is the most popular social website in the UK, the fourth most-accessed site in the UK and the second in Ireland, and similar sites are mushrooming throughout the Internet. MySpace is the best known, but Orkut, Facebook, Xanga, Friendster and many others have scores of millions of users worldwide.

With so many young people involved, it is no wonder that sometimes things go wrong, awfully wrong. We have all read headlines like: 'NZ teen sells drugs through Bebo', '13-year-old Californian girl victim of intense abuse through MySpace', 'Belfast authorities dismayed at sectarian violence found in some Bebo sites', 'Dublin rapists lure girls to party with Bebo', 'Misuse of Facebook forces college in New Jersey to expel student'. The concern expressed by parents and educators, then, can hardly be called surprising.

Apart from worrying, many parents are puzzled. What's the attraction in this alternative universe? 'Because it's fun!' according to Michael Birch, founder of Bebo. Perhaps there's little more to it than that. Teenagers and young adults love sharing stories, showing off pictures, making comments and gossiping, making friends, listening to each other's playlists, watching funny video clips made by their mates, and so on.

If it is only a matter of fun, social networking websites are, at least, incredibly addictive. Young people can spend hours in one sitting

trawling through their favourite pages. Now that they can also watch videos posted on the site, users have access to hours of entertainment while waiting for replies to their comments. The time wasted is incalculable. One teenager posted a wail of regret: 'Why, oh why was Bebo ever invented? I don't even want to think about how many hours of my life it has now consumed.' At least she was honest.

How should parents react?

These sites are here to stay. Therefore, parents and educators alike cannot afford to bury their heads in the sand, especially if these novel means of communication have so great an influence on the young people in their care. The alternative is surrendering their education and safety to God knows who.

The lurid side of websites like Bebo and MySpace has been widely reported – young

continued over

continued from previous page

people receive or gain access to inappropriate material, become vulnerable to bullying, can easily fall into the clutches of predators, and so on. Under pressure from media and parents, companies like Google, which owns Orkut, MySpace and Bebo, have been implementing safety measures to minimise the abuse.

But even if it were possible to shelter young people from the bullies and criminals, there is a more insidious problem inherent in the medium: living on social-networking sites impairs the formation of young people's character:

- They foster curiosity, vanity and jealousy. The sites basically constitute a gigantic popularity contest.
- They encourage dishonesty: you can provide any age that suits your purpose, and you can fantasise about your weekend – who is to know what really happened?
- Users tend to live in their own little world, and excessive use can make them forget how to behave properly in the company of others.
- They discourage deep and reflective thinking – not to mention proper spelling and punctuation.
- Most importantly, they become a real obstacle to genuine empathic communication.

Although many teenagers now use social networking websites to make friends, they miss out on a key aspect of genuine friendship, which is empathic communication. At a computer screen, using broken and coded language, you cannot see, hear or touch, or experience the feelings of another person. Even webcams are hardly a substitute for a face-to-face relationship. This feature could ultimately have serious implications for the future of society. It is important nowadays to foster face-to-face relationships in the home and elsewhere: having meals together or going on outings with family and friends, playing team sport or even just watching TV together and discussing it afterwards.

Such are the realities, though, of this phenomenon, so it must be asked: what can concerned parents do? A lot – but don't expect it to be easy. First of all, teenagers should be warned of the dangers. A few horror stories are usually sufficiently intimidating to deter a youngster from providing a phone number or address and other personal information to strangers, or accepting as friends on their site people they have never met. Parents should also learn how to access the site. This isn't spying; they are just reading what millions of strangers are also reading. If a child knows that her mum or dad is savvy enough to take a look, they might think twice before posting or sharing inappropriate material. As shock therapy, try calling your child to breakfast one morning by her MySpace username and see how she reacts.

Luison Lassala is director of Anchor Youth Centre in Dublin, and is a freelance IT consultant
luisson@aonanach.com

QUESTIONS

(i) What, in your view, is the writer's attitude to the Bebo phenomenon as revealed in this article? Support your answer by reference to the text. **15**

(ii) From your reading of this article, what did you learn about the positive and negative aspects of social-networking websites? **15**

(iii) Do you find the style of writing in this article appealing? Support your answer by detailed reference to the text. **20**

ANSWERS

COMMENTARY

(i) I would argue that the writer is more precautious of this social-networking phenomenon than a fan of it commencing by declaring it a national wonder in both the UK and Ireland illustrates its enormous popularity, in particular amongst the youth, 'the most popular social website in the UK ... and the second in Ireland'.

Commentary: cautious?

The writer acknowledges the obvious attractions of the site, giving the reader a tour around the accessories, which have heightened its adoration. Here, he clearly recognise its positives and understands its appeal to the modern teenager.

Commentary: A poor choice of word. 'Popularity' might have been better.

Commentary: its positive aspects

This attitude fluctuates as the writer informs the reader of the hidden dangers and safety issues which are apparant. They highlight the trap many youngsters fall innocently into when revealing personal information and uploading unsuitable material. This evidently allures sexual predators and caters for bullying which the writer emphasises 'become vulnerable to bullying, can easily fall into the clutch of predators ...'

Commentary: a poor choice of word

Commentary: apparent

Commentary: lures

continued over

In addition, the writer is aware of the addiction of the site and how it encourages young people to waste valuable time reading useless, sometimes vile information. They also remark on how the site is growing as a barrier between real face-to-face relationships and regrets that this is the least quite upsetting, 'miss out on a key aspect of genuine friendship'.

addictive qualities

becoming a barrier to

The student has read and understood the question, and provides a reasonably accurate summary of the writer's viewpoint. However, the answer is quite poorly written, making it an unclear and confusing reading experience. As noted above, the student misuses many words and phrases. She would, perhaps, have been better advised to use simple, ordinary language to make her point. **8/15**

(ii) Following my reading of this article I became aware of both the positive and indeed the negative aspects of social networking websites. It is evident that these sites are entertaining, interesting and useful for keeping in contact to the modern teenager.

Juxtaposing such however, it permits young people to spend hours ploughing through pointless information and attaining material of a vulgar content. It caters for bullying and this can severely deteriorate the self esteem of a person. It accommodates internet predators to obtain personal details and creates a situation whereby the user is put in danger, and for the most part they are innocently oblivious to this.

damage a person's self-esteem

allows

It allowed me to realise the masked insecurities of the internet in particular in relation to Bebo as it is very open to the sharing of information. It recalls how physical, face-to-face relationships with friends and family degenerates when young people become obsessed with 'cyber-talk'. They tend to lose touch with reality, with living circumstances and become overly addicted to talking through a keyboard. It constitutes curiosity, vanity and jealousy amongst users and encourages dishonesty.

unnecessary use of this word

Overall, the site does prove to behold many attractive features to it, diverging this however the article does highlight and emphasise the sites negative effects.

have

Again, the student addresses the question but is let down by the clarity and quality of the writing. She manages to outline what she has learnt from the piece, but does so in a manner that is clumsy and confusing to read. As noted above, the student misuses a number of difficult words, and would have been better advised to use ordinary, simple language to clearly make her point. **8/15**

(iii) Yes, I did find the writer's style of writing appealing. The writer was successful in conveying concrete facts to the reader in a concise manner. The opinions expressed were done so in an ordered fashion, they did not come across as biased or untrue.

The use of headings such as 'How should parents react?' enables the reader to obtain soloutions to the problems associated with the site, and such soloutions are advised in the form of bullet points. Doing so, allows a more focused approach, it is laid out more clearly and thus is more striking. The use of these bullet points strengthens the writer's opinions, they stand out and are illuminated in the readers memory, as they too are very important.

solutions

solutions

poor choice of word

The writer asks questions and proceeds with a reply. Personally, I find this method of conveying relevant information extremely intelligent as they are usually questions which the reader holds in mind, such as 'what can concerned parents do?'

No doubt after reading such an informative and educating article on their children's safety on the internet, parents will be keen to take action. Answering this question delivers this information.

continued over

ANSWERS

The writer concludes the article in a humerous tone, travelling down the famous route of parents embaressing their children, this defenitely strengthens the appeal of the piece to the target audience.

COMMENTARY

humorous

embarrassing

definitely

Once again, the student addresses the set task. The writing is of a slightly higher standard than in the previous two questions, but still leaves something to be desired. The student could have earned a higher grade by using simpler language and short, clear sentences. Only use words and phrases that you understand and can deploy correctly. **12/20**

Total mark 28/50 (C3)

SAMPLE ANSWER 3

The moral cost of video games

By Matthew Devereux

In the controversial new video game 'Manhunt 2', the player is required to sneak up behind innocent victims, hit them over the head with a garden spade, and then use that same weapon to decapitate them. The whole thing is pretty graphic because the game has, well, pretty graphics. As blood gushes, you're supposed to feel satisfied that you're ready for the next challenge.

To some, this scenario captures everything wrong about video games. 'They're too violent,' detractors say. 'And they glamorise violence. Children might be tempted to copy them.' While this is an understandable concern, it misses other inherent problems with many video games today: primarily, an utter lack of moral consequence.

Countless studies have tested the alleged links between virtual violence and its real counterpart. Conclusions vary, but I certainly don't need a panel of academics with statistics, reports and surveys to explain to me that the teen across the street isn't going to attack me with a garden spade. Still, if you're a parent, the sheer intensity of violence in many games today ought to be a valid concern. You wouldn't let your children view online pornography, so why let them decapitate people in a video game?

Yet many parents buy their children games rated inappropriate to their age group. Why? Perhaps it's a hangover attitude from the 'Pac-Man' past, when all video games were presumed to be harmless fun. Or maybe they just want their kids to think they're cool. Who knows?

Years ago, after the tragic shootings in Columbine, the news media were quick to lay blame at the game-industry's door, among other easy targets such as the music industry. But what is surprising about the media's obsession with violence in games is that it overlooks more serious lapses in values. By concentrating on the bloodthirsty and dramatic, they're ignoring influences that are much more harmful to children long term. Take, for instance, the idea of ruthless competition, that for every winner there are necessarily losers. Regardless of what game you're playing, the message is almost always the same: do whatever it takes to win, even at the expense of everyone else.

Imagine if that were the moral of every movie and TV show you ever watched. Would the world be a better or worse place? Would you let your children play a game that promoted such a dog-eat-dog mentality? Fundamentally, most games operate within a moral framework: good versus evil (or vice versa). But what games conspicuously lack is moral consequence. Once you've killed someone, stolen something, or blown up a building, that's usually the end of it – you'll rarely get to see the emotional impact of your actions on the characters around you.

Every bit of mayhem becomes just another item on a video-game to-do list. Games ignore moral consequence and emotional nuance to focus on the purely visceral. There are only two types of decisions you can really make: the strategically correct one or the strategically incorrect one. There is no 'right' or 'wrong' – only success or failure.

Unbridled competition combined with no moral consequence eventually leads to a lack of compassion. And without compassion, humanity is lost. What games then risk instilling, not just in kids, but in anyone who plays them, is a kind of sociopathy: a deficiency of conscience. Whether this might be imitated outside of gaming is beside the point. What we should be asking ourselves is if we really want to spend ever-more time playing things that encourage these values. That's a moral question, one that's easily sidelined in favour of simply having fun, but it's something we all must consider as the pastime grows more popular.

QUESTIONS

(i) Do you think the first paragraph provides an effective opening to this piece? Give reasons for your answer. **10**

(ii) What negative consequences of video-gaming does the writer identify in this article? **20**

(iii) In this piece, the writer attempts to persuade us that video games have negative consequences. What features make this an effective piece of persuasive writing? **20**

ANSWERS

COMMENTARY

(i) In my opinion I think the opening paragraph is a good introduction to the matter being addressed. From what I perceive, this article is aimed at parents of young children and I feel that the opening paragraph, illustrating a typical scene in the game, is significantly effective in grabbing reader's attention and giving them an example of how horrific platform gaming has become.

Long, poorly constructed sentence.

The use of words such as 'decapitate' and 'gush' help to introduce the types of violence being depicted in this game, making the reader fully aware of why it is so 'controversial'. Furthermore, the writers description of the victims being 'innocent' aids him in creating somewhat of a biased towards the video game by putting across the impression that the victims portrayed in this murderous scene were normal, average people but yet this games objective is to bash and decapitate them with a spade and also to acquire just satisfaction from your actions.

Another long, badly written sentence. The student should have used a number of shorter sentences to make his point clearly.

With these points in mind, a reader of this article would be put in the exact frame of mind that the writer perceives which allows them to make just his accusations and also to take his side in this very serious article about violence in video games.

Yet another long, poorly constructed sentence!

The student has been asked to say whether or not he thinks the opening paragraph of the text is effective. His answer is overly long and poorly written. Though the student makes some valid points and much of his answer is relevant, he loses a lot of marks for incoherency and poor grammar. He would have been better advised to make two or three short points and back them up with reference to the text. **4/10**

(ii) The writer mentions various consequences of the playing of violent video games, firstly the fear of young children replicating the actions portrayed by characters in their fictional games.

Yet again, the student writes a long, convoluted and badly constructed sentence. He should have definitely used two sentences here.

In the second paragraph of this article, the writer illustrates how 'children might be tempted to copy them' referring to the fact that game developers are 'glamorising violence' and so children feel there is no wrong to be done in imitating what they see and do in the game.

Long, poorly constructed sentence!

The writer also refers to the shootings in Columbine and makes the reference that the gaming industry was to blame for the series of events and that the problems that fueled the killers' motivation may have been desensitisation due to their exposure to violent video games.

Lastly the author also examines the possibilities that video games are affecting children in the long term by subjecting them to 'the idea of ruthless competition' and also the 'lack of moral consequence'.

continued over

ANSWERS	COMMENTARY
These two issues, the writer feels, are less talked about and therefore are more prevalent to become a major problem as children who play violent video games develop. For ruthless competition we read that the idea that there is only 'one winner, everyone else are losers', is one that is often portrayed in various games leading to an image coming across that you must do everything and anything possible to win 'even at the expense of everyone else'.	What two issues? The student has made at least three different points above. The student appears incapable of writing short, coherent sentences.
For the issue of moral consequence, the writer argues that games are causing children to be in the mind set that they can do what ever they want, no matter how bad and not be punished for their actions. In their games they are rewarded for their wrong doing without being shown the aftermath or effects of their actions in the game, an issue which the author feels needs to be addressed in great seriousness.	Yet again, the student has written a long, convoluted answer that lacks proper focus. The student uses plenty of relevant material but fails to make clear points. His answer meanders and is difficult to read. He should have made three or four basic points and used appropriate quotes from the text to back them up. **9/20**
(iii) The authors attempt to persuade the readers of this article are very well put forward and he does so by using a variety of different methods and techniques.	
Firstly the carefully chosen language he has used. In the article words such as 'decapitate', 'gush' and 'brutal' are used to depict the scene being described. The words are all linked with violence and gory scenes and so help the reader to both visualize and also examine how horrific the actions of the characters in the various video games can be.	
Also the writer uses his reader's emotions and fears against them as he literates how if you are a parent and you are not showing 'valid concern' towards the violence in video games than you could be classed as a 'bad parent' for letting your children be subjected to this violence and not caring, the 'hangover attitude' as the writer describes it.	awkward construction Long, rambling and poorly constructed sentence, containing numerous grammatical and syntactical mistakes.

We also see evidence of this feature whereby the writer very cleverly contrasts letting children be subjected to violence with letting children be subjected to pornography, expressing how can it be wrong to do one but not the other. This again is playing with the mind as the writer lays the seed of doubt in his reader's minds almost telling them that by subjecting their children to games with mature content they are bad parents.

The student is making a good point here, but is let down again by his inability to write clear and concise sentences.

Lastly, the writer's use of questions. By inserting questions is his article he is forcing his readers to answer them and therefore question there own lives to see if they are really doing what is right for their children. Questions such as 'would you let your children play a game that promoted such a dog-eat-dog world?' again lay a seed of doubt which develops in the readers mind to make them believe that video games in the genre depicted in this article should not be viewed by children and if it is the reality that they are than you as a parent are no better than the game designers themselves.

Too long, too convoluted, too difficult to read.

Once again, the student has failed to write in a clear and concise manner. He has clearly read and understood the question, and, yet again, his answer contains some relevant points and includes appropriate references to the text. However, he is continuously haemorrhaging points by using sentences that are long, poorly constructed and almost impossible to read. The lesson to be learnt here: use short, simple sentences to make clear, concise points. That way you will be guaranteed high marks if your material is relevant. **10/20**

Total mark: 23/50 (D)

SAMPLE ANSWER 4

Text messages destroying our language

Eric Uthus, *Washington Daily*

I have speculated on this for many years, but it seems to have finally come true: mobile phones are evil. That is, grammatically speaking.

In a report released from the State Examination Commission in Ireland, our ability to write in English is slowly deteriorating. And the main culprit behind this deterioration, believe it or not, is text messaging. According to this report, all those messages you send your friends and family at work, on the bus or during class are leading to a weaker understanding of correct grammar and spelling. We are forming shorter sentences, using simpler tenses of verbs and, worst of all, little or no punctuation.

I knew this was coming. From the first time one of my friends sent me the message 'I've got 2 go, talk to U later,' I knew the end was approaching like black clouds foreshadow the storm. The English language as we once knew it is out the window, and replacing it is this hip and cool slang-induced language given to taking the vowels out of words and spelling phonetically.

I'm glad they finally found something to blame 4 this mess. For a long time, I thought ppl had just become lazy and didn't want to take the time or effort to write complete and coherent sentences. But, apparently, it's the technology itself causing the downfall of writing.

Forget the fact that most mobile phones these days have the option to use T9 or similar technologies that will spell words 4 U, making txt msging even faster. Some people don't have a 2nd to spare; they have jobs, classes and people to luv, so contemplating the time it takes to write correctly seems ridiculous when the information they wish to pass on can be done so quicker.

I guess I feel kinda like a hypocrite, because I remember reading old English novels and thinking, 'Man, I can't believe people actually wrote like this! This is soooooo boring and goes on forever.' But now, here I am, complaining that people are writing in a way that I can't appreciate.

Maybe it's coz I'm afraid of the fast-paced society we live in, which is partly 2 blame 4 the breakthrough of txt msgs. We are always on the run, never stopping to say 'Hi!' or have an actual conversation. Instead, we send a couple of words to tell people that we still luv them. But really, who looks at 'I <3 you' and feels loved? Or worse yet, has ne1 actually laughed out loud when they claimed that they were LOL?

Yet, what's really sad about the deterioration is that it doesn't appear to bother us. Which brings up the question: where is the line going 2 be drawn? At what point do we begin to realise that our language, something that can be beautiful, eloquent and can paint pictures to rival da Vinci's, is almost in the can? Has txt msging begun a downward spiral that will bring about the end of good writing? Can you imagine reading a good novel with its narrative in text speak? Can you imagine reading Hemingway or Tolstoy as a txt msg?

I hope that this report from Ireland gets more attention and leads to some serious discussion among the populace. As small as this issue may seem, it has a bigger impact on the way we communicate than most people care to admit. I can't, of course, speak for you, but I can't bear to see just how far the destruction can go. I hope U feel da same way.

QUESTIONS

(i) What negative consequence of text messaging does the writer highlight at the beginning of the piece? **10**

(ii) In this piece, the writer uses abbreviations common in text messages, for example, '4U' instead of 'for you'. What effect does this device have on the impact of his article? **10**

(iii) 'I hope you feel da same way'. Do you agree with the writer's point of view? Support your answer with reference to the text. **30**

ANSWERS

(i) According to this article, text messaging is hastening the decline in English spelling and grammar. Uthus writes that people's ability to write in English is deteriorating slowly, leading to a weaker understanding of correct grammar and spelling. To save time, people compact their words and sentences in order to send a more concise message, at the expense of the English language. The writer believes that the inclusion of 'hip and cool slang-induced language given to taking the vowels out of words and spelling phonetically' into our everyday lives will be destructive to the English language.

(ii) Uthus' method of incorporating abbreviated terms into this article is highly effective in helping the reader to understand why he believes texting is a negative mode of interaction. The abbreviations fit easily into the text, and serve to illustrate vividly how young people might make similar mistakes within school exams, due to their mis-education via text.

Uthus also makes a very good point about the use of 'LOL' within texts when people purport to be expressing their feelings. There is, as the author notes, an increasing sense of falseness created within young people, which could lead onto a widespread epidemic of shallow, wilful adults. Using the abbreviated text serves to effectively illustrate and reinforce the point he is making.

COMMENTARY

The student clearly addresses the question, and her answer is entirely relevant and backed up by appropriate references to the text. She writes well, displaying a good vocabulary and a strong command of English. Her answer is of adequate length and, most importantly, to the point. **10/10**

Again, the student addresses the question she is being asked. Her answer is focused, and what she writes is entirely relevant. She makes appropriate reference to the text, and her answer is well structured, comprising of two paragraphs, each with distinct points. **10/10**

(iii) I believe the writer makes some very good points in relation to how dangerous texting is to the future of grammar. What Uthus terms a 'weaker understanding of correct grammar' could lead to a decline in one's education in general. One's diction is very important in creating first impressions in future job situations as well as with general acquaintances.

However, the writer believes 'the English language as we knew it is out the window' and this is a bad thing. But the English language, and all other languages, have evolved throughout the ages. They continue to change spelling, add new words, as well as omit vocabulary that has come into disuse. The English language has incorporated many words from different areas to increase understanding of ideas through language, like the French words 'avant-garde' and 'déjà vu'. Some people may have a sense that this is 'bastardising' the English language, but the use of these words has become commonplace, and we now look on the inclusion of these words as normal.

In more recent times, the 'Americanizing' of words has been seeping into the English books on this side of the Atlantic. 'Zs' are being used more often when 'Ss' would have traditionally been used, for example, 'initializing' rather than 'initialising'. In Chemistry, the 'ph' in sulphur has now been changed to 'f', keeping in line with our American counterparts. The English language is evolving, and terms like 'LOL' and spelling words phonetically will probably become part of our future English classes.

It is a fact that the English language will evolve, but is this necessarily a good change? This is what Uthus is asking his readers.

In this question, the student is being asked to give her own opinion and she does this. She makes specific points about the arguments put forward by the writer, and clearly outlines her point of view. The answer displays a keen awareness of the issues that the article raised, and the student has written a well-structured response using well constructed sentences and paragraphs that are perfectly sequenced and well managed. **30/30**

Total mark: 50/50 (A1)

SAMPLE ANSWER 5

Sudden pots of gold leave Irish with identity crisis

New York Times

Between sips of café latte and laments about the staggering cost of property, the Irish are asking themselves: Who do we want to be as a country now that we have all this money? 'We are certainly in new territory,' said Joseph O'Connor, the best-selling Irish novelist who wrote *Star of the Sea*. 'We haven't been here before.'

It was not at all long ago that Ireland was a threadbare nation – barely relevant in European affairs. Finding a job then meant hopping aboard an aircraft out of the country. People counted their pennies and not their commuter miles, and poverty, for many, was an ever-stubborn component of Irish life.

But Ireland's jump into the European Union coupled with aggressively pro-business economic policies changed all that. In little more than a decade, the so-called Celtic Tiger was transformed from one of the poorest countries in Western Europe to what's now one of the richest in the world. Its gross domestic product per person, not quite 70 per cent of the EU average in 1987, sprung to 136 per cent of the EU average by 2003, while the jobless rate sank to 4 per cent from 17 per cent. And *The Economist* then cemented Ireland's powerhouse reputation by declaring it the country with the best quality of life in the world.

However, that new status is bringing with it an identity crisis, one that is forcing the country, and its government, to grapple with the flip side of wealth. While few would say Ireland was better off 20 years ago, some are beginning to point out that national wealth alone does not necessarily bring happiness.

Irish newspapers have been filled with accounts of the pitfalls of growth, secularisation and wealth, some of them trivial, a few of them serious: suicide is at record levels, divorce is increasingly common, property prices are soaring, traffic is horrendous, personal debt is spiralling. Even the high cost of a cup of coffee has become a lightning rod, prompting people here to label the country 'rip-off Ireland'.

A survey released by a market-research group, Mintel Ireland, even revealed that most people did not feel their lifestyle had improved in recent years, primarily because the cost of living had exploded with any rise in opportunity and earning. Another study pointed out that stress levels throughout Ireland were ballooning to proportions never before seen in the country.

Emily O'Reilly, the government's ombudsman and information commissioner, fanned the debate in a speech bemoaning Ireland's values in the wake of its economic success and flourishing secularisation. 'Many of us recoil at the vulgar-fest that is much of modern Ireland,' she said. 'Divorce was meant to be for the deeply unhappy, not the mildly bored. Sunday shopping was supposed to be a convenience for the harassed worker, not a new religion.'

The speech drew both applause and derision, with many saying Ms O'Reilly was succumbing to the Irish penchant for gloom. O'Connor, the writer, said a degree of reflection and self-criticism was welcome, but not if it spoiled the party altogether. Artists, for example, were thriving; there were more writers, painters, poets and musicians than ever before. 'Yes, people are commuting long distances now. But not nearly so long as the commute to, say, Australia, which is where many people had to go to find jobs a generation ago.' But, he added good-naturedly: 'If Ireland is the best place to live, God help us.'

QUESTIONS

(i) 'the flip side of wealth'. According to this article, how has Ireland's economy changed in recent times? **15**

(ii) From your reading of this article, what did you learn about the negative consequences of this economic change? **15**

(iii) The writer sets out to inform the reader about recent changes in Ireland and the different attitudes to the changes. What features make this an interesting piece of informative writing? **20**

ANSWERS

(i) The writer of this article describes the Ireland of the past as a 'threadbare nation' which was unable to give its population good quality livings or house everyone in appropriate accommodation. People had to travel to America and Australia in order to lead lives that were not surrounded by poverty. Nowadays, there is an excess of wealth in Ireland. Our inclusion in the European Union has promoted us from being a dependent nation to a self-sufficient one. Ireland is now one of the wealthiest countries in the world and, in turn, after being aided by the EU, we are now aiding poorer countries. The article provides statistics comparing Ireland's past unemployment rates to the present situation, and indeed, the Celtic Tiger roared exultantly during our economic expansion. A reduction of 13% in the numbers of the unemployed is a significant victory, with 4% being one of the lowest unemployment rates found in the world. This is a far cry from the poverty-stricken days of the 1840s.

COMMENTARY

This sentence is too long and should have been broken up into shorter sentences.

Unless you are quoting from the text itself, don't look to impress the examiner with flowery language. Just answer the question as clearly as possible.

The student has been asked to describe how, according to the article, Ireland's economy has changed in recent years. The answer he gives is entirely relevant and focused. He begins by describing how poor the country was before, and goes on to show, with appropriate reference to the article, how the economy has changed. However, the answer suffers from some poor grammar and one or two clumsy sentences. **12/15**

(ii) 'Money cannot buy happiness'. This saying is the crux of this article in dealing with the 'flip side of wealth' in Ireland. The writer lists the 'pitfalls of growth', stating that suicide has increased, divorce is becoming a norm, personal debt is soaring outrageously due to the absurdly high prices of property, and the price of material goods sold in Ireland have lead us to be called 'rip-off Ireland'.

awkward sentence

As well as this, there is increasing competition for jobs and promotions, leading to an increase in stress in the lives of people living in Ireland. What is more, values among people seem to be decreasing, as along with the wealth, there seems to be less belief in religion and more focus on material needs. This 'flourishing secularism' can be seen through the increase in divorce cases. Divorce is a decision made more easily today than ever before, as Emily O' Reilly says: people seem to be getting a divorce due to boredom rather than due to more serious reasons.

society's values are suffering

The answer is adequate: it answers the question and makes a number of appropriate references to the text. However, it again suffers from some awkwardly constructed sentences that make the student's answer difficult to read. Perhaps the student would have been better advised to use simpler language to make his points clearer. **12/15**

(iii) This article is a very good example of informative writing as it lays out each piece of information logically, leading each point onto the next. Ireland of the past is compared with the present situation and the pros and cons of such changes are dealt with fluidly, increasing the reader's understanding of the case with ease. The writer also gives statistics to back up the points made, giving the article an overall appearance of well-researched and informed writing. This allows the reader to understand and believe what is written. It also adds a touch of humour, ('If Ireland is the best place to live, God help us') which engages the reader, giving a sense of satisfaction after reading the piece.

The student would have been better advised to use two sentences here, e.g. 'I think that this article is a very good example of informative writing. The writer makes his points clearly, and they flow in a logical fashion.'

The student makes some good points about informative writing, and his answer is focused and relevant. However, the student could have made better use of quotes. Once again, the student's answer is let down by poorly constructed sentences. It is generally best to write short, clear sentences. **14/20**

Total mark: 38/50 (B)

SAMPLE ANSWER 6

Humanity's Impact on the Planet

QUESTIONS

(i) Write **one paragraph** that would serve as an introduction to this collection of images entitled, 'Humanity's Impact on the Planet'. **10**

(ii) Which of the images makes the strongest impact on you? Give a reason for your answer. **15**

(iii) If asked to select another image to expand this group of images depicting 'Humanity's Impact on the Planet', what image would you suggest? Give reasons for your choice. **25**

(i) Now for the weather: Temperatures across the globe will rise and Ireland and Britain will be hit by a growing number of tornadoes over the coming years, while Indonesia will be victim to another tsunami. Cases of skin cancer may rise in Australia due to the expansion of the hole in the ozone layer, while countries in milder climates will enjoy a variety of seasons each week, whether it is summer or winter. Humanity has had such an intense effect on the planet's environment, global warming is now threatening our own way of life. Change is coming to our planet, 'weather' we like it or not.

The student has read and understood the question. Her answer is entirely appropriate and is well written. The student's decision to use the device of the weather report is very effective, and displays good imagination. **10/10**

(ii) The image with the sign 'Due to flooded footpaths you may not be able to complete your journey' is a very good indication of where we are going as a world, in relation to the weather. It is becoming increasingly difficult to combat the destructive effects of the weather due to its changeability. Paths one was once able to walk are made impassable, and soon, whole areas will be submerged due to the global rise of sea-levels.

Humanity is having such an effect on the world's health that we are endangering our own as well. Interchangeable seasons should not become a norm, but this is what we are witnessing – heat-waves in winter and floods during the summer. With the aid of films like 'The Day After Tomorrow' and 'An Inconvenient Truth', more attention is now being given to caring for our environment. In order to prevent more situations like the one depicted in this picture, people are starting to be more aware of fuel emissions, recyclables, and many other possible preventative measures in order to slow down the effects of global warming.

The student begins by addressing the question but her answer soon becomes less a discussion of the image and the impact it has had on her, and more of a general discussion of the consequences of environmental damage. Though her answer is well written, it could be argued that much of what she writes is not entirely relevant to the question being asked. The student might have been better advised to have made greater reference to the picture and its features, and to have stated why it had such a strong impact on her. **10/15**

(iii) Adding a picture of a source of renewable energy to the collection above would show productive ways of combating global warming. Pictures of wind turbines, or solar panels on houses can show us that there are alternative methods by which we can replace our dependence on fossil fuels with renewable energy. What is more, using these alterative energy sources will reduce the cost of electricity, create healthier living environments by reducing dangerous gases in our homes and therefore can benefit people as well as the planet. In this way humans can find ways to work with the planet, rather than having such a bad effect on it.

Once again, the student begins in a manner that shows she has read and understood the question. However, while she makes good points about renewable energy sources, she could have said more about her choice of picture in relation to the other pictures. For example, she might have said that the pictures presented above paint an entirely negative image of humanity, and that the inclusion of a picture of renewable energy sources would illustrate the fact that some people are working towards a better future. It could also be argued that given the fact that 25 marks are being awarded for this question, the student's answer is not long enough. **15/25**

35/50 (B3)

SAMPLE ANSWER 7

The Cost of Living

QUESTIONS

(i) Select **one** of the visual images in this collection for the front cover of a book entitled 'The Cost of Living'. Give reasons why you consider your chosen image to be the most effective and/or suitable. **15**

(ii) Which of the images makes the strongest impact on you? Give reasons for your answer. **15**

(iii) If asked to select another image to expand this group of images depicting 'The Cost of Living', what image would you suggest? Give reasons for your choice. **20**

ANSWERS	COMMENTARY
(i) For the front page of a book entitled 'The Cost of Living', I would choose the image of the woman shopping. It is not that the image fits the stereotype of the female shopper, with her children, and the spending of money on trivialities. Rather, it shows the general truth of the job required by a mother in this case, how in the consumer-driven world of today, people have to spend more for less.	Though she has clearly read and understood the question, her answer is too short. She could have given more reasons for her choice of image. As it stands, she gives one rather awkward reason that does not explain in a satisfying way why such an image would be appropriate for the proposed book. With 15 marks going for this question, it would be appropriate to give at least two clear reasons for the choice you make. **6/15**
(ii) The image that truly hits home to me is the picture of the starving little girl. This picture, shown in conjunction with the images of money wastage, drives home the fact that we are wasting our money on trivialities, material possessions that do not fully constitute our future happiness. This girl would be truly happy if she knew she would be having three meals a day, every day. Whereas, many people in the developed countries seek to find happiness by spending money through impulse buying. Not only that, we, who have so much money, are not fully considering that every cent should count for something.	The student has again clearly read and understood the question, beginning with a sentence that demonstrates this. She follows this with a good reason for her selection. However, it could be argued that the latter part of her answer displays a lack of focus. Her remarks about developed countries draw her away from the task at hand, i.e. a discussion about a particular image. The student should have made at least one more point about the impact the picture has had on her. **7/15**
(iii) I believe an image depicting war would also be of good to the group of images in displaying 'The cost of living'.	An awkward sentence.
Though it may not seem relevant superficially, it calls to mind the amount of money dedicated to war, at the expense of our economy. The United States of America are now experiencing a serious downward shift in their economy due to the mass amounts of money invested into war, which shows few signs of stopping. Is this what living costs? With each bomb costing over a million dollars to produce, the States are literally blowing up their own money, and the health and educational systems are the ones that suffer. Being such an influential country, the economies of the rest of the developed countries are feeling the effects of this downturn and we ourselves will come to know how to save the pennies, as they say.	In keeping with her answers to the other questions, the student demonstrates that she has read and understood the question. However, she yet again fails to give a number of reasons for her choice, and instead gets sidetracked by issues not entirely relevant to the question asked. Her discussion of American investment in arms, while being well written, takes her away from the task at hand. This loss of focus, combined with a poorly written opening sentence, means the student loses a lot of marks here. She should have made a number of clear points about her selection of image and its appropriateness to the collection above. **10/20**
	Total mark: 23/50 (D)

SAMPLE ANSWER 8

The Man of the World

by Frank O'Connor

When I was a kid there were no such things as holidays for me and my likes, and I have no feeling of grievance about it because, in the way of kids, I simply invented them, which was much more satisfactory. One year, my summer holiday was a couple of nights I spent at the house of a friend called Jimmy Leary, who lived at the other side of the road from us. His parents sometimes went away for a couple of days to visit a sick relative in Bantry, and he was given permission to have a friend in to keep him company. I took my holiday with the greatest seriousness, insisted on the loan of Father's old travelling bag and dragged it myself down our lane past the neighbours standing at their doors.

'Are you off somewhere, Larry?' asked one.

'Yes, Mrs Rooney,' I said with great pride. 'Off for my holidays to the Learys.'

'Wisha, aren't you very lucky?' she said with amusement.

'Lucky' seemed an absurd description of my good fortune. The Learys' house was a big one with a high flight of steps up to the front door, which was always kept shut. They had a piano in the front room, a pair of binoculars on a table near the window, and a toilet on the stairs that seemed to me to be the last word in elegance and immodesty. We brought the binoculars up to the bedroom with us. From the window you could see the whole road up and down, from the quarry at its foot with the tiny houses perched on top of it to the open fields at the other end, where the last gas-lamp rose against the sky. Each morning I was up with the first light, leaning out the window in my nightshirt and watching through the glasses all the mysterious figures you never saw from our lane: policemen, railwaymen, and farmers on their way to market.

I admired Jimmy almost as much as I admired his house, and for much the same reasons. He was a year older than I, was well-mannered and well-dressed, and would not associate with most of the kids on the road at all. He had a way when any of them joined us of resting against a wall with his hands in his trouser pockets and listening to them with a sort of well-bred smile, a knowing smile, that seemed to me the height of elegance. And it was not that he was a softy, because he was an excellent boxer and wrestler and could easily have held his own with them any time, but he did not wish to. He was superior to them. He was – there is only one word that still describes it for me – sophisticated.

I attributed his sophistication to the piano, the binoculars, and the indoor john, and felt that if only I had the same advantages I could have been sophisticated, too. I knew I wasn't, because I was always being deceived by the world of appearances. I would take a sudden violent liking to some boy, and when I went to his house my admiration would spread to his parents and sisters, and I would think how wonderful it must be to have such a home; but when I told Jimmy he would smile in that knowing way of his and say quietly: 'I believe they had the bailiffs in a few weeks ago,' and, even though I didn't know what bailiffs were, bang would go the whole world of appearances, and I would realise that once again I had been deceived.

It was the same with fellows and girls. Seeing some bigger chap we knew walking out with a girl for the first time, Jimmy would say casually: 'He'd better mind himself: that one is dynamite.' And, even though I knew as little of girls who were dynamite as I did bailiffs, his tone would be sufficient to indicate that I had been taken in by sweet voices and broad-brimmed hats, gaslight and evening smells from gardens.

Forty years later I can still measure the extent of my obsession, for, though my own handwriting is almost illegible, I sometimes find myself scribbling idly on a pad in a small, stiff, perfectly legible hand that I recognise with amusement as a reasonably good forgery of Jimmy's. My admiration still lies there somewhere, a fossil in my memory, but Jimmy's knowing smile is something I have never managed to acquire.

QUESTIONS

(i) With reference to the text, describe Larry's view of Jimmy. **25**

(ii) Do you find this style of writing appealing? Support your answer with reference to the text. **25**

ANSWERS

COMMENTARY

(i) Larry sees many different views of Jimmy. The one he notices the most though and admires him for is his elegance and his classiness. Larry realises Jimmy is from a well to do family and is much more fortunate in his upbringing, but still sees him as a friend. Jimmy is well mannered, well dressed and has brought to this a well-bred smile a knowing smile.

poor opening sentence

very poor sentence

As elegant as Jimmy seems, Larry knows he is an excellent boxer and wrestler. Larry saw this air about Jimmy, though of superiority and sophistication. Larry knew Jimmy could have taken anybody and watched time after time as he refused. Larry saw a man of mind, authority and class.

awkward, poorly constructed sentence

To Larry, Jimmy seemed a man of intelligence, authority and class.

Jimmy grew up with many advantages coming his way. His appearance was clean and crisp. He was well spoken. Jimmy knew what he was talking about when he made such a bold statement. Larry did not envy this but was often deceived by Jimmy's appearances. Larry has always respected Jimmy and admired him although it has faded somewhere in his memory.

Poor choice of words. The student might have said that Larry was clean-cut and well-dressed.

Not only is this sentence poorly constructed, the point it makes is simply not true. At no point in the story is Larry 'deceived' by Jimmy's appearance.

The paragraph is poorly written and rambles aimlessly.

Though the student seems to have grasped the question, she fails to make clear and coherent points. Not only that, but her references to the text are weak and, on one occasion, entirely misconceived. Her sentences are frequently badly constructed and her choice of words and phrases poor. Her paragraphs lack structure and fail to contain a clear point. **10/25**

ANSWERS	COMMENTARY

(ii) No, I don't really find this type of writing appealing.

The author does use some very good descriptive language. His explanations of how the streets looked, Jimmy's house, his stature and appearance are beautiful. He captures the images perfectly in the reader's mind in order for them to produce a picture in their heads.

description

The student began by saying this type of writing does not appeal to her. Now she says it is 'beautiful'!

strange, poorly constructed sentence

The author's style of writing in my opinion aims more for the older adult who would have experienced these harsh times. The author referring to nineteen forty's nineteen fifty's urban Dublin when the classes in Ireland were undeniable noticeable.

refers

poorly expressed

For a modern reader, unless you're really interest in history you would find it very hard to read. So far there is no momentum in the story. There is nothing gripping the reader to want to read more.

awkwardly written, poor choice of words

It appears to be a biography out of a section of the author's life. He's taking a segment out of his childhood and relaying it back to us. As a reader of today it is not appealing to us as there is no action, no suspense, no drama. There is none of the intriguing themes.

History and looking back at old Ireland does not appeal to me as it does not concern me. It had nothing to do with me nor I to do with it. A biographical text of a man that made no major imposition of how Ireland got where it is today in my opinion would not appeal to many readers as it is neither here nor there.

The student begins by stating a clear point of view, thereby indicating that she has read and understood the question. However, having said that she does not find the writer's style of writing appealing, she immediately goes on to say that the author uses some 'good descriptive language' and that his descriptions are at times 'beautiful'. She then confuses the subject matter of the story with style. Her point about the story being irrelevant to a young reader of today is not really appropriate to a question about style. However, she does return to the writer's style and makes some good, relevant points, saying that the story lacks momentum, action, suspense and drama. Having said that, her answer is poorly constructed and lacks a clear aim. It is brave of her to say that she does not find the writer's style appealing, but she muddles her own point of view by instantly praising the writing. **12/25**

Total mark: 22/50 (D)

SAMPLE ANSWER 9

from *The Architecture of Happiness*

by Alain DeBotton

A few years ago, caught out by a heavy downpour, with a couple of hours to kill after being stood up for lunch by a friend, I took shelter in a smoked-glass-and-granite block on London's Victoria Street, home to the Westminster branch of McDonald's. The mood inside the restaurant was solemn and concentrated. Customers were eating alone, reading papers or staring at the brown tiles, masticating with a sternness and brusqueness beside which the atmosphere of a feeding shed would have appeared convivial and mannered.

The setting served to render all kinds of ideas absurd: that human beings might sometimes be generous to one another without hope of reward; that relationships can on occasion be sincere; that life may be worth enduring ... The restaurant's true talent lay in the generation of anxiety. The harsh lighting, the intermittent sounds of frozen fries being sunk into vats of oil and the frenzied behaviour of the counter staff invited thoughts of the loneliness and meaninglessness of existence in a random and violent universe. The only solution was to continue to eat in an attempt to compensate for the discomfort brought on by the location in which one was doing so.

However, my meal was disturbed by the arrival of thirty or so implausibly tall and blond Finnish teenagers. The shock of finding themselves so far south and of exchanging glacial snow for mere rain had lent them extremely high spirits, which they expressed by unsheathing straws, bursting into ardent song and giving one another piggy-back rides – to the confusion of the restaurant staff, who were uncertain whether to condemn such behaviour or to respect it as a promise of voracious appetites.

Prompted by the voluble Finns to draw my visit to a precipitate close, I cleared my table and walked out into the plaza immediately adjacent to the restaurant, where I properly noticed for the first time the incongruous and imposing Byzantine forms of Westminster Cathedral, its red-and-white-brick campanile soaring eighty-seven metres into the foggy London skies.

Drawn by rain and curiosity, I entered a cavernous hall, sunk in tarry darkness, against which a thousand votive candles stood out, their golden shadows flickering over mosaics and carved representations of the Stations of the Cross. There were smells of incense and sounds of murmured prayer. Hanging from the ceiling at the centre of the nave was a ten-metre-high crucifix, with Jesus on one side and his mother on the other. Around the high altar, a mosaic showed Christ enthroned in the heavens, encircled by angels, his feet resting on a globe, his hands clasping a chalice overflowing with his own blood.

The facile din of the outer world had given way to awe and silence. Children stood close to their parents and looked around with an air of puzzled reverence. Visitors instinctively whispered, as if deep in some collective dream from which they did not wish to emerge. The anonymity of the street had here been subsumed by a peculiar kind of intimacy. Everything serious in human nature seemed to be called to the surface: thoughts about limits and infinity, about powerlessness and sublimity. The stonework threw into relief all that was compromised and dull, and kindled a yearning for one to live up to its perfections.

After ten minutes in the cathedral, a range of ideas that would have been inconceivable outside began to assume an air of reasonableness. Under the influence of the marble, the mosaics, the darkness and the incense, it seemed entirely probable that Jesus was the son of God and had walked across the Sea of Galilee. In the presence of alabaster statues of the Virgin Mary set against rhythms of red, green and blue marble, it was no longer surprising to think that an angel might at any moment choose to descend through the layers of dense London cumulus, enter through a window in the nave, blow a golden trumpet and make an announcement in Latin about a forthcoming celestial event.

Concepts that would have sounded demented forty metres away, in the company of a party of Finnish teenagers and vats of frying oil, had succeeded – through a work of architecture – in acquiring supreme significance and majesty.

QUESTIONS

(i) How does the author view the interior of the cathedral, in relation to the restaurant? Support your answer with reference to the text. **20**

(ii) What is the author's attitude to the people within the restaurant, on evidence of this passage? **15**

(iii) In terms of description, choose a sentence within this passage and explain why it appeals to you as a reader. **15**

ANSWERS

COMMENTARY

(i) The clear contrast between the descriptions presented by the author, of the restaurant and the cathedral convey the authors views aptly. To begin with, the author sees the interior of the cathedral as being strikingly unique. His attention to detail in his description portrays a noteworthy image in the readers mind. Personally, I feel that the author was taken back by the cathedral to such an extent that he will never forget it. Such features as the mosaic of 'Christ enthroned in the heaven' caught the author's eye and were certainly unique. In relation to the restaurant the interior was mundane and all that could be seen were the 'brown tiles'. Pole apart from this dull ordinary sceptical, the appearances of the cathedral seemed unparallel to the author.

A slightly awkward opening sentence. Could have been better written.

Not the best sentence and not entirely relevant either.

aback

poor sentence and word choice

The interior of the cathedral was obviously awe-inspiring to the author. The final line describes how he feels a new strength and ability to contemplate certain issues after viewing the building. In relation to the restaurant, which failed to inspire him in any way, the cathedral injected a wave of surprising emotions into the author, leaving him with the view of it as a miraculous place of wonder.

The cathedral appears to be, as described in this text, a place that is full of meaning and importance. 'The stonework threw into relief all that was compromised and dull'.

continued over

ANSWERS

When comparing this to the restaurant we see that all that has been lost in the world of consumerism, has been maintained within the cathedral. To the Author it is still pure and unspoiled and the natural features of the interior reflect this. The symbolic language contained within the statues and mantle are deep in sacred meaning.

COMMENTARY

awkward sentence

poor sentence

The student's answer, while generally relevant to the question asked, lacks focus and involves too many flawed and poorly constructed sentences. The length of the answer is appropriate to the marks being awarded, but the student has failed to organise his answer into clear paragraphs with a logical flow. Instead, the answer tends to ramble and is dissatisfying to read. The student does make some relevant points and, to his merit, relates the author's view of the cathedral to the restaurant, but these points are lost in a body of text that is muddled and, at times, incoherent. **10/20**

(ii) With regard to the customers in the restaurant the author views them as over-worked, unfriendly, monotonous characters. Warped by the social discomfort and commercial inhumanity that plagues society they are happiest when self-contained in their own bubbles, only concerned with eating, working and basic human requirements. 'Customers were eating alone, reading papers or staring at the brown tiles, masticating with a sternness and brusqueness beside which the atmosphere of a feeding shed would have appeared convivial and mannered'.

This sentence is overlong and poorly written. The student is attempting to use complicated language when clear and simple language would have served him better.

The author sees the 'blond Finnish teenagers' as being rowdy, disorderly and perhaps inconsiderate as they entered the restaurant, and excited after the sight of rain took over the space in a barbaric and uncivilised manner. This attitude is clearly to be seen when he vacated the premises. Also the last lines indicate to us that the poet sees the youths as almost a hindrance to society. They prevent people like himself to appreciate the world and to contemplate life.

Again, the student has used an overly long sentence.

writer

appreciating

contemplating

'Concepts that would have sounded demented forty metres away in the company of a party of Finnish teenagers and vats of frying oil', finally, in the brief description that the author presents to us, of the staff in the restaurant we gain an insight into his image of them. The staff appear to have fallen victim to the same mundane, lifeless behaviour of the customers. At the first sight of abnormal behaviour they become almost disorientated and misplaced. From the line 'uncertain whether to condemn such behaviour or to respect it as a promise of voracious appetites', we see how they long to break free from the monotonous behaviour of their jobs.

Long sentence that is difficult for the reader to follow.

poor choice of word

This answer, while focused and relevant, is poorly written. The student uses unnecessarily long sentences, which are difficult to read. He would have been better advised to write short sentences and make clear points. **8/15**

(iii) The sentence which I find particularly appealing is 'drawn by rain and curiosity, I entered a cavernous hall, sunk in tarry darkness against which a thousand votive candles stood out, their golden shadows flickering over mosaics and carved representations of the stations of the cross'. It appealed to me in many ways but primarily in its excellent use of imagery. The image of the long hall, which appears endless, drew me as a reader into the comprehension, inviting me to read on. The image of the hall added a mysterious quality to the cathedral, injecting curiosity into me as a reader.

The repetition of this phrase is unsatisfying.

I found this line particularly interesting because of the author's stark contrast between light and dark. The image of the dark, gloomy corridor, illuminated only by the flickering candles, is very appealing to the senses with regard to the eye or the ear. We can almost hear the candle flames flickering and the sound of the rain drops.

These words are unnecessary and make the sentence weak.

The majesty and nuance of the language used by the author in this sentence grabbed my attention. This sentence contained a memorable musical quality, which adds greatly to the overall rhythm of the piece. The assonance of the letter 'o' in 'stood out their golden shadows' slowed the piece down dramatically and indicated the contrast between the mayhem of the restaurant and the tranquillity of the church.

The student's answer is focused. He selects a sentence and says why it appealed to him, just as he was asked to do. He makes some valid points and gives good reasons for his selection. The third paragraph, in particular, is very good. However, the answer contains a few weak and flawed sentences, and the repetition of the 'me as a reader' in the opening paragraph is tedious. The length of the answer is appropriate, and the paragraphs are well structured. **13/15**

Total mark: 31/50 (C3)

6 Letters

There are two types of letter that you need to know about: formal letters and informal letters.

[Sender's Address]
Address Line 1
Address Line 2
Address Line 3
Address Line 4

Letter Date

[Recipient's Address]
Address Line 1
Address Line 2
Address Line 3

Dear [Name]:

Subject line that gives subject of letter

The first paragraph of the letter should get straight to the point and explain the purpose of the letter. All paragraphs should be set apart by skipped lines. Avoid making your paragraphs too long.

The second paragraph develops the subject of the letter. Its length will depend on what the letter is about.

The third paragraph develops the subject of the letter. Its length will depend on what the letter is about.

The closing paragraph is usually one or two sentences long, and will generally thank the recipient for taking the time to read the letter.

Yours Sincerely [if you know the recipient's name]
Yours Faithfully [if you don't know their name]

Enclosure: (X) [Indicate how many items enclosed]

THE FORMAL LETTER

This is one of the most common styles in current use.

There are many scenarios in which you should use formal letters, but among the more common are job applications, letters to government bodies, letters of complaint, and letters of thanks to corporate or charitable organisations. It is important that you produce something approximating to the above format in the Leaving Cert.

Invariably, the advice to correctors is to reward students who reproduce the *rubrics* (or general conventions) of the letter format. It stands to reason that if you produce the letter format perfectly, you will get all the marks available for this.

THE INFORMAL LETTER

Back when God was a boy, people wrote letters to each other all the time. Since then, the advent of e-mail has pretty much tolled the death knell for the informal or personal letter.

Nobody has told the Department of Education about this, however, so from time to time, informal letters form the basis for answers in Paper 1. Consequently, even though the skills involved in personal letter writing are about as contemporary as those involved in hunting your dinner with a stick, it is useful to give a brief indication of what informal letter writing involves.

In this regard, the main thing you need to know is that informal letters are far more relaxed than formal letters. Because you will be personally acquainted with the recipient of the letter, there is no need to pay too much attention to stylistic and formal conventions. On the whole, if you produce something like this sample, you should be okay.

It's as easy to write a letter that is formally correct in all of its details as it is to write one that isn't, so you might as well familiarise yourself with the conventions associated with both types of letter.

[Sender's Address]
Address Line 1
Address Line 2
Address Line 3
Address Line 4

Letter Date

Dear [Name],

First paragraph. The first paragraph is indented underneath the salutation. Usually, paragraphs are divided in informal letters by way of an indent rather than a skipped line, but there is no hard-and-fast rule about this.

Second paragraph. Often, personal letters will give a narrative of events in the sender's life. If so, divide each significant event into a paragraph.

Third paragraph. By now, the general format of a personal letter should be clear, though be aware that an informal letter is a personal document, so you have far more latitude in how it is structured that you do with a formal letter.

Yours Sincerely,
Signature

P.S. For some odd reason, people feel obliged to put in a postscript in personal letters. Only do this if you have genuinely forgotten to include something in the main text.

SAMPLE ANSWER 1 FORMAL LETTER

Write a letter to an author that you admire explaining why you admire them and inviting them to speak at your school. (Note: This is an answer to a Question B)

Sunnyvale
Ballyhooley
Co. Cork
Tel No. 021-4772599

3rd March 2010

Mrs Stephanie Meyer
Square Hill
Palmerstown
Dublin

Dear Mrs Meyer,

I am writing to you in order to congratulate you on the success of your trilogy. 'Twilight', 'New Moon' and 'Eclipse' are my favourite books, and I really admire you for daring to bring an old-fashioned love story, with a modern twist, back onto the market. I am a great fan of yours. I feel my whole school would benefit from hearing how you made these books what they are today.

I would like to invite you to speak in my school, Colaiste Na Toirbhirte. It would be an honour to have you speak to my fellow classmates and I know, for some of them, they will enjoy your Twilight Trilogy as much as I did.

If you have any questions or are interested in speaking at the school, please don't hesitate to write to the above address or telephone.

Thank you for your time, and I wish you every success in the future.

Yours sincerely,

Lisa Peterson

Lisa Peterson

This sentence is too long and is poorly constructed.

This could perhaps be better phrased.

MARKS & COMMENTARY

CLARITY OF PURPOSE

The student has clearly read and understood the question. She has been asked to accomplish two tasks: tell the author why she likes her and invite her to her school. Both are accomplished. Everything in the letter is relevant to, and focused on, these aims. Nothing irrelevant or distracting is introduced.

The student has been asked to write a formal letter, i.e. to a person she does not know. She shows that she understands what a formal letter is, and reproduces the conventions of the genre. **14/15**

COHERENCY OF DELIVERY

The student uses a register appropriate to the task, and maintains it throughout the letter. The material is arranged in a coherent sequence, and the sentences and paragraphs flow logically from one to the other. **14/15**

EFFICIENCY OF LANGUAGE USE

This letter has a level of vocabulary more than adequate to the task, and a nice variety of sentence structure. Yet, perhaps the student could have taken the opportunity to insert more lively and interesting phrases when praising the author's work.

The student should have placed the last sentence of paragraph 1 at the start of paragraph 2, and so ensure that each paragraph had a distinct topic. As pointed out above, there are two overly long, poorly constructed sentences, which detract from the coherency of the work as a whole. **10/15**

ACCURACY OF MECHANICS

The student's spelling and grammar are good. **4/5**

Total mark: 42/50 (B1)

FOCUS ON LANGUAGE STYLES

This letter features some good informative writing. The student gives the author information in a clear, concise fashion. It also features some mildly persuasive writing. The student tells the author how her fellow students would benefit from a visit by her to the school.

SAMPLE ANSWER 2 FORMAL LETTER

Write a letter to the manufacturer of the video game 'Manhunt 2' complaining about the negative effects violent video games are having on society.(Note: This is an answer to a Question B that relates to the Comprehension text 'The Moral Cost of Video Games' in the above Comprehension chapter.)

Mr Richard Roberts
Kinsale,
Co. Cork
Ireland

Tuesday 11th March 2010

Mr Jack O' Brien
C.E.O of game development and design,
Rockstar Games,
5th Avenue,
New York City,

Dear Mr Jack O' Brien,

I am writing this letter in relation to upcoming release of the controversial 'Man Hunt 2'. This game, like its predecessor has been banned in more than thirty countries worldwide due to its graphic nature and horrific plot in which, I am told, the characters main objective is to hit and decapitate innocent victims with a spade.

Having researched the game and its content, I feel that it is unreasonable and unjust to bring out such a game and subject it to an audience that is not fit for its viewing. Games like this are causing numerous problems for children today. It causes them to re-enact the malicious scenes depicted in the game, to lose their sense of right from wrong and forget the consequences of undergoing such actions in the real world.

I feel that the game depicts a dog-eat-dog world where a man's only choice is to kill viciously and be rewarded for his efforts. Also the game portrays a message that is lacking moral consequence and allowing children to believe they can commit various horrific acts of murder and not be justly dealt with for their actions.

I hope that you realise what your game will be subjecting children to. Also I hope you reconsider your previous statements in recent press releases as to when the game will be available to the public to give you time to reconsider and think about what your game could do to our young population. The massacre at Columbine was just the tip of the iceberg; do really wish to be at the centre of another massacre? I will leave the choice up to you….

I look forward to your reply,

Yours sincerely,

Richard Roberts

The last part of this sentence is unclear and badly written. Something simpler would have been more effective: perhaps 'and target it at children'.

undertaking

This sentence is too long and poorly written. It would read better if it was broken into two shorter sentences: 'The game's message is an immoral one. It allows children to believe that they can commit horrific acts of murder without moral consequence.'

Again, this sentence is too long, making it somewhat clumsy and ungainly.

MARKS & COMMENTARY

CLARITY OF PURPOSE

The student has clearly read and understood the question. He has been asked to perform one task: complain to the producers of a violent video game. This is accomplished. Everything in the letter is relevant to, and focused on, this clear aim. Nothing irrelevant or distracting is introduced.

The student has been asked to write a formal letter, i.e. to a person he does not know. He shows that he understands what a formal letter is, and reproduces the conventions of the genre, including addresses, salutation and sign-off. **14/15**

COHERENCE OF DELIVERY

The student uses a register appropriate to the task, and maintains it throughout the letter. The material is arranged in a coherent sequence and the sentences and paragraphs flow more or less logically from one to the next.

The student refers to one real-world example, the Columbine massacre. Though this is a short letter, perhaps one or two more examples and references could have been fitted in to reinforce the student's core point. **12/15**

EFFICIENCY OF LANGUAGE USE

This letter has a level of vocabulary adequate to the task and varies the structure of its sentences enough to prevent the reader becoming bored. The letter also works from a 'paragraphs and punctuation' point of view. There are no serious punctuation errors, and the letter is quite well-paragraphed, with each paragraph focusing on a different aspect of the student's complaint.

However, as pointed out above, there are a number of overly long and poorly constructed sentences, which seriously detract from the coherency of the work as a whole. From a vocabulary standpoint, several words are misused or poorly chosen. **8/15**

ACCURACY OF MECHANICS

The student's spelling and grammar are generally good. **4/5**

Total mark: 38/50 (B2)

SAMPLE ANSWER 3 INFORMAL LETTER

Write a short letter to a friend in which you describe your preparation for the Leaving Cert exams.

3 Riverbrook,
Sneem,
Co. Kerry.

Dear Carol,

How is the study going? I'm really starting to feel the pressure now that the Leaving Cert is just around the corner. Did you follow my suggestion and make out a timetable? I've found it invaluable, as I feel like I'm really progressing through all the subjects. I have also set deadlines for myself so that I can reach a certain point in my revision each week. If you want to try a similar approach to me, try to have a sample paper for the English exam done by Friday and we could check each other's answers when I call over that evening.

Even with our 'beautiful' Irish weather, I find walking is a great way to take a break from all the learning. Otherwise I'd overload my brain! Playing the guitar for five or ten minutes really helps relax me if I get stressed as well. I'd say you're making use of the piano in your home as well!

Let me know if you want me to bring any notes over at the end of the week, and I'd really appreciate your help with my disastrous attempts at probability in maths!

See you then,

Mary.

MARKS & COMMENTARY

CLARITY OF PURPOSE

The student has clearly read and understood the question. She has been asked to write an informal letter describing how her preparation for the Leaving Cert is going, and she does just this, perfectly reproducing the conventions of the genre.

Everything she writes is relevant to the task. She maintains focus throughout. **15/15**

COHERENCE OF DELIVERY

The student uses an informal, chatty tone and register that is entirely appropriate, and she maintains this throughout the letter. Her ideas are well managed, and the references to study and methods of relaxing are perfect. The letter flows nicely, with each paragraph following logically on from the last. **15/15**

EFFICIENCY OF LANGUAGE USE

This piece features some vibrant and lively use of language, which is appropriate to the task. There is a decent level of vocabulary, and the sentence patterns are varied enough not to bore the reader. Her ironic mentioning of the 'beautiful' weather, and the expression 'overload my brain' are well used and appropriate to this informal, friendly letter.

The letter makes good use of paragraphs, with each paragraph focusing on different aspects of the student's preparations for the exams. **15/15**

ACCURACY OF MECHANICS

Though this is an informal piece of writing, the student never departs from conventional grammar and syntax. Her spelling is accurate throughout. **5/5**

Total mark: 50/50 (A1)

SAMPLE ANSWER 4 FORMAL LETTER

The *Irish Times* is looking for a film critic to write a weekly column. Write a letter applying for the position.

12 Castle Avenue
Blackrock
Cork City
Phone: 021 4567478
30th August 2010

The Personnel Manager
The Irish Times
Dame St.
Dublin 1

Dear Sir or Madam,

I am writing to apply for the post of film critic as advertised in the Irish Times of August 23rd. I have just attained a B.A. from University College Cork in English and History. I am currently working as an apprentice sub-editor on the Evening Echo and am hoping to eventually pursue a full-time career as a columnist.

As you will see from my enclosed CV, I wrote a weekly column for both my college and school newspapers. In secondary school I wrote on cultural topics, such as television, book and film reviews, starting in my transition year and continuing up until the Leaving Certificate. This experience enabled me to write for the university paper, where my journalism was focused entirely on cinema, reviewing the latest movie and DVD releases.

Length of sentence causing confusion.

I believe that my five years' experience of writing weekly columns has given me the necessary knowledge and familiarity that would enable me to fill the advertised role. I am accustomed to writing to a deadline and have solid computer and editing skills. Needless to say, I am a keen and enthusiastic cinema-goer, and believe I possess a sound knowledge of cinematic history that enables me to write about the topic with confidence and depth.

which qualifies

which

I enclose my CV along with two letters of recommendation, and would be glad to forward on a folio of my journalistic work.

Thanking you in anticipation, I remain,

Yours faithfully,

Robert Hayes

MARKS & COMMENTARY

CLARITY OF PURPOSE The student shows a clear understanding of the task involved. All information given in this letter is relevant to the topic at hand, that is, writing a serious letter in the hopes of impressing a prospective employer. However, using terms like 'cinema-goer' may not be appropriate. **14/15**

COHERENCE OF DELIVERY The student gives a clear and relevant account of his work experience, relaying information in a practical and easy-to-read manner. His tone is perfect for a job-application letter, showing deference as well as confidence in his ability. **14/15**

EFFICIENCY OF LANGUAGE USE There are few errors in syntax within this letter. However, the sentence, 'In secondary school I wrote on cultural topics, such as television, book and film reviews, starting in my transition year and continuing up until the Leaving Certificate', is too long and not the easiest to read. Control of sentence structure is necessary in a letter attempting to impress a future employer. However, the paragraphs are well structured.

In general, the student displays a reasonable level of vocabulary. **13/15**

ACCURACY OF MECHANICS The student's spelling and grammar are good. **5/15**

Total mark: 46/50 (A1)

7 Reports

Reports present information. If the information they present is new (and it usually is), they may also recommend that some course of action be taken in the light of this information.

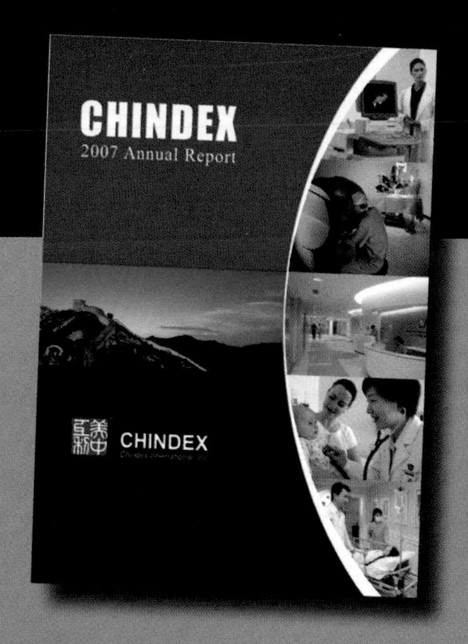

CONTENT

The text of a report will be divided into the three categories of *introduction, discussion* and *recommendations*. On paper, a report will thus look something like the following:

TITLE The title of the report.

AUTHORS The company, group or individual who has written the report.

RECIPIENT The company, group or individual for whom the report is written.

DATE The date of publication/submission of the report.

INTRODUCTION The introduction to the report clearly sets out the problem that the report is supposed to address or the purpose for which it was chartered. Keep it relatively brief, and maintain clarity of expression at all costs.

DISCUSSION The discussion is the main body of the report. It will deal with things like how the report gathered its data, resolved problems and made its analyses. This part of the report will be a bit longer than the introduction and the recommendations, and will represent the bulk of your effort.

RECOMMENDATIONS Most reports make a number of recommendations on the basis of their research. Always phrase these as suggestions (rather than instructions), and arrange them in bullet-point format. This section should be relatively short.

SAMPLE ANSWER 1

Write a short report for a government agency outlining the role that social-networking sites are playing in young people's lives. (Note: This is an answer to a Question B and relates to the Comprehension text, 'Beating the Bebo Addiction', in the Comprehension chapter above.)

Aim of this report

The aim of this report is to examine the role that social-networking sites are playing in young people's lives. It will raise some possible concerns about these networking sites and propose measures that might be taken to safeguard teenagers?

A revolutionary method in communication

A new type of communication behaviour has emerged among young people in a few short years, in which they explore their identities and build relationships. Social-networking sites create a space for youths to communicate with friends and peers, share information on current trends, but also on personal information.

Possible problems

These young people are learning from each other how to use these sites, without parental supervision, generating their manners and morals from the examples of other inexperienced youths, rather than learning from parents or teachers. They are pouring their minds into cyberspace, dislocating themselves from face-to-face relationships.

This is a worrying trend that is increasing in popularity, with sites like Bebo and Facebook becoming some of the most popular sites visited on the Internet.

Unsupervised access to these sites can leave a youth open to harassment by other children online, or they may be victim to sexual predators, who could take advantage of the personal information shown on each youth's individual page. There is also evidence that inappropriate material is circulating through these social-networking sites.

Proposals

Informing teenagers that prospective employers and university officials, as well as parents, can check out their 'private' pages may lead teenagers to become more guarded with the information they post on the websites. Advice ought to be given to teenagers regarding the safe usage of such sites. Such advice might include the following:

- Use the particular site's privacy settings and only share personal information with family and trusted friends;
- Do not have pictures of yourself on your profile; upload a favourite animal or flower instead;
- List the nearest large city instead of the small town you live in;
- Use a nickname or pseudonym instead of your full name.

Warning students should be our main priority in dealing with this veritable 'Pandora's Box'. Closing the lid on personal information is of the utmost import in protecting young people from harm.

MARKS & COMMENTARY

CLARITY OF PURPOSE

The student has clearly read and understood the question. She has been asked to write a report outlining the role that social-networking sites are playing in young people's lives. In her answer, she does just this, perfectly reproducing the conventions of the genre. She clearly outlines her aim in the 'Aim of this Report' and the information she presents in subsequent paragraphs is entirely relevant to the report. The student maintains focus throughout

One possible criticism of this report is that it fails to state how the material was gathered; nor does it refer to any sources for its information. **13/15**

COHERENCE OF DELIVERY

The student uses formal tone and register that is entirely appropriate. She organises her information in a way that is clear, logical and easy to read. The references to Bebo and Facebook are entirely appropriate, and her paragraphs are well structured and managed. The use of bullet points when giving her recommendations is commendable, and allows the information she is presenting to be easily grasped. **15/15**

EFFICIENCY OF LANGUAGE USE

A report needs to be informative. The student has used language that is clear, measured and entirely appropriate to the task. Though she raises legitimate concerns in the report, she does not use melodramatic or alarmist language. There is a decent level of vocabulary, and the sentence patterns are varied enough not to bore the reader. The report makes good use of paragraphs and headings. **15/15**

ACCURACY OF MECHANICS

Her spelling, grammar and syntax are accurate throughout. **5/5**

Total mark: 48/50 (B1)

FOCUS ON LANGUAGE STYLES

As stated above, a report ought to use language that is informative. The student should avoid giving personal opinions and base his or her advice on facts and verifiable information. The above answer is a good example of an informative answer. It is clear and easy to read, and the main points are easily comprehended. As already mentioned, the student's one failing was that she did not make any mention of where the information in the report came from.

SAMPLE ANSWER 2

There is much discussion as to whether or not young people are being exploited by advertisers. Write a short report to the Advertising Standards Authority outlining your views on the matter.

We must recognise that, by definition, all advertising contains an element of exploitation. All people have certain needs that are unavoidable and are attainable only with the purchasing power of money. Therefore, advertisers are perfectly justified in marketing their goods with a view to fulfilling these basic and intrinsic needs.

unnecessary repetition

Difficulties arise when it becomes clear that advertisers are clearly going beyond this baseline, and are instead generating unnecessary desires on the part of consumers. This activity is of particular concern when it comes to considering younger people.

this

long sentence, but well controlled

Given the country's recent economic boom and the rising levels of affluence amongst young people, it is inevitable that advertisers will target that sector of society in the hope of capturing potential life-long costumers for particular goods and services.

between

loss of control in sentence

It would appear from research carried out by social psychologists that people aged from 14–21 are particularly vulnerable to peer pressure. In terms of consumerism, this manifests itself in the need to feel constantly supplied with the latest line of goods that they feel their friends are acquiring.

A very obvious example of this is the marketing of mobile phones. In spite of the fact that all phones provide the basic minimum services of texts and phone calls, the leading mobile-phone companies relentlessly push the latest upgrades in the technology by using advertising that generally employs good-looking, 'trendy' young people seen with the latest gadget or gizmo.

into / purchasing

necessarily

This form of marketing may lead to certain individuals feeling pressurized (in)to purchase(ing) the advertised product, in spite of the fact that they may not necessary(ily) have the disposable income with which to do so. The decision to purchase arises solely from the need to maintain an up-to-date self-image that is dictated largely, if not entirely, by the manipulation of advertisers.

taking advantage of

In conclusion, the challenge for the Advertising Standards Authority lies largely in being able to distinguish when certain advertisers overstep the mark between providing basic needs, and begin to manipulate the weaknesses and vulnerabilities of young people in order to maximize profits.

MARKS & COMMENTARY

CLARITY OF PURPOSE The student instantly loses marks for not structuring his answer properly. This is a report and should, therefore, establish its aim clearly at the beginning. The piece reads more like an article or personal essay at times. Introducing the report to the Advertising Standards Authority would have been a good start rather than launching straight into it. The student should also have made clearer proposals at the end of the report. That said, what the student does write is relevant. His reference to recent research is well used. **11/15**

COHERENCE OF DELIVERY The paragraphs are well laid out and flow logically. The example of the advertising of mobile phones is great. The student uses an appropriately formal tone throughout. **14/15**

EFFICIENCY OF LANGUAGE USE The student displays a good level of vocabulary, and varies his sentence patterns. The piece is broken up into well-constructed paragraphs. **14/15**

ACCURACY OF MECHANICS The student's spelling and grammar are of a high standard. **5/5**

Total mark: 44/50 (A2)

8 Advertisements

Short advertisements are most often encountered in newspapers and magazines, where they appear on the bottom left or bottom right of a page containing reports or articles. Their central purpose is to advertise an event or product in a quick and effective way.

CONTENT

MAKE AN IMMEDIATE IMPACT

When writing ads of this type, your first task is to make an immediate impact. The product or service being sold needs to be presented in as striking and as attractive a way as possible. This is best achieved by having a large headline that is followed by some attractive sentiment about the product being advertised. Sometimes, this sentiment can be expressed in a witty or clever way.

MAKE A SERIES OF BRIEF POINTS

Most people don't consciously choose to read advertisements, so you need to make the most of the short period for which you will have the reader's attention. Use bullet points to emphasise the most important features of the product or service. Doing this will guide the reader's eye to the essential information that you want them to register.

INCLUDE A BRIEF 'MISSION STATEMENT'

A short 'mission statement' should either precede or follow the information communicated in the bullet points. This statement will articulate the general philosophy of the company or organisation that sponsored the ad, and will use the words 'we' and 'our' a lot.

KEEP THE TONE POSITIVE

In terms of tone, a short ad must be relentlessly optimistic. Your whole task is to convince the reader that their life will be immeasurably improved if they just buy your product, so always emphasise the positive. As far as advertising is concerned, there is no such thing as an unsolvable problem.

SAMPLE ANSWER 1

Based on your reading of the piece, write the text of an advertisement offering guided tours around Westminster. (Note: This is an answer to a Question B that relates to the Comprehension text above, an extract from Alain DeBotton's *The Architecture of Happiness*.)

London is an international capital steeped in culture, and attracts millions of visitors each year. If you are considering taking a trip to this fascinating city, one experience, that should not be missed is London's own Westminster Cathedral.

Probably not the best words to describe a visit to a cathedral.

This cultural and religious centre is attractive to people of all ages. With its alabaster statues of the Virgin Mary set against rhythms of red, green and blue marble, and its stunning mosaics, this is truly an architectural masterpiece that inspires feelings in its visitors that are unparallelable anywhere else in the city. Be it spiritual guidance or wonder and awe at this spectacular building, visitors to the Cathedral leave feeling refreshed and revived. This is a rare experience and opportunity in today's hectic society, and gives people the chance to realign themselves.

The Cathedral runs a number of guided tours on weekdays, which will aid you in your experience of Westminster. Our experienced guides will give a brief history as they lead you through this magnificent building.

Several different packages are available offering everything from day retreats to thirty-minute tours. In summer months we have tours on the hour, in an attempt to facilitate visitors.

Better to say that 'Audio sets are also available.'

Also audio sets are available in several different languages such as French, Spanish and Japanese for those who request them. These sets give a detailed description of all regions of the Cathedral from the majestic ten-metre-high crufix to the many mosaics which feature here.

Prices range between three and ten pounds for forty-five minute tours which group day trips costing extra. The audio headsets cost five pounds for an hour-long tour. Bookings can be taken on line or for further information regarding tours please call 0044 7755288376.

A visit to Westminster Cathedral has benefits beyond description, benefits that will effect you spiritually and emotionally and that will leave you with countless memories.

Get your taste of paradise with Eden Holidays

Have you had enough of boring travel agents who never quite give you the holiday you want? Here at Eden Holidays we specialise in catering for every conceivable choice of holiday destination. Whether you want to languish by the beach in a tropical paradise or immerse yourself in the icy splendour of the Antarctic, we have the holiday for you.

WHY TRAVEL WITH EDEN?

- **We have been in the business of holiday provision for over fifty years, and have an unrivalled database of international contacts**
- **We offer the best prices and group deals available anywhere in the world**
- **We include insurance as part of our prices**
- **We will assign you an individual consultant with whom you can plan an itinerary that suits YOUR needs and interests, not ours.**

At Eden, we pride ourselves on our rapport with our customers. For us, holiday provision is not a business – it is a vocation. Call us or view our website for a sample of what we have to offer.
We guarantee you won't be disappointed.

Phone: 1234567 Web: www.eden.org
Mail: eden@mail.com
Eden Holidays, Dublin 2

MARKS & COMMENTARY

CLARITY OF PURPOSE

The student has been asked to write an advertisement for tours around Westminister Cathedral and she handles the task quite well. She shows that she understands what an advertisement is, and reproduces the conventions of the genre. She uses persuasive language that appeals to the reader, enticing them to consider the service she is advertising.

It could be argued, however, that the student fails to highlight the virtues of tours themselves, focusing instead on the architecture of the cathedral. As this is an advertisement for the tours and not specifically the cathedral itself, the student would have been better advised to say early on why these tours should not be missed. **11/15**

COHERENCE OF DELIVERY

The student uses a tone and register appropriate to the task, and maintains it throughout the advertisement. She has sequenced her paragraphs reasonably well, beginning with an introduction to the cathedral before moving on to some of its features, and ending with clear information about the service that the text is advertising. Her references and examples are appropriate, and she makes good use of the text that this question is based on. **13/15**

EFFICIENCY OF LANGUAGE USE

This piece features some vibrant, positive language, which is vital to an advertisement. Her paragraphs are reasonably well managed, each containing a separate, easily understood point. The punctuation in the piece is generally good, though some of the sentences could be better constructed. The student could also have used some punchier language, especially at the beginning of the advertisement, to grab the reader's attention and sell the service. She also would have been better advised to use bullet points to clearly convey some of the features of the tours. **11/15**

ACCURACY OF MECHANICS

Grammar and spelling are reasonable. Mistakes have been highlighted above. **3/5**

Total mark: 38/50 (B2)

FOCUS ON LANGUAGE STYLES

This piece of writing is a fairly good example of the language of persuasion. The writer uses appropriate words and phrases that suggest a visit to the cathedral will be a special experience. She frequently uses sensational language and exaggeration, describing the building as 'stunning' and 'not to be missed'. Suggesting that a visit to the cathedral provides a welcome relief from the pressures of modern living is a good appeal to the reader's emotions.

SAMPLE ANSWER 2

Imagine you are running for the position of Student Council President in your school. Compose an informative election leaflet encouraging students to vote for you. It should outline your own leadership qualities and the changes you would like to introduce into your school.

spelling

repetition and spelling

leading?

The student should just have said, 'I will push for'. Saying 'I will aim to push for' is not strong enough.

awkward phrasing

VOTE FOR ROBERT PATCH AS YOUR NEW STUDENT COUNCIL PRESIDENT!

As President of the Student Council, I promise to serve the needs of all students faithfully and to the very best of my ability. I believe I can bring many good qualities to the position, and have, during my years in the school, shown that I possess the credentials necessary for the job.

In my second and third year I was secretary of the Student council and so, therefore, posses invaluable experience of how the council operates. As head of the school debating team, I led our group of speakers to the final of the National School debating final in 2006. On the sports field, I have been vice-captain of the hurling team for the past two years and am confident that I can play my part in helping the squad to victory this coming year.

As your President, I will aim to push for many necessary changes in the school that will enhance the quality of our educational experience. Amongst the proposals I intend to introduce are:

1. **An increase in the amount of PCs in the school's computer room in order that more students can access the Internet for educational purposes.**
2. **With the same purpose in mind, I wish to see the introduction of wi-fi facilities in the student common room for students with laptops.**
3. **Greater channels of communication made available between teachers and students in order that individual pupils can express any difficulties they may be having. To this end, I would like to see each teacher make available an hour each week in order to meet with any student who has issues concerning course material or other issues that they may wish to discuss.**

These are only a few of the proposals I intend to launch in order to make our school a better place for all of us. In order for this to come about, I ask you for your vote in the coming elections. Thank you!

MARKS & COMMENTARY

CLARITY OF PURPOSE

This is a good example of an election leaflet. The student stays focused on his goal, and everything he writes is relevant to the task at hand. The leaflet is a form of advertisement, and the student recognises the need for persuasive language. He could, however, have used punchier language and made some clearer points. As it is, the leaflet is not quite as urgent and attention-grabbing as it ideally ought to be. **12/15**

COHERENCE OF DELIVERY

He has organised his paragraphs well, which ensures that the leaflet is logical and easy to follow. The register is appropriate to the task. 12/15

EFFICIENCY OF LANGUAGE USE

Some of the student's sentences are a little weak; for example: 'I would like to see each teacher make available an hour' is an awkward way to dictate your wishes. Rather, 'I would like to request that teachers will keep an hour free each week for students in need of aid'. The student does, however, use a variety of sentence patterns, thus ensuring that the piece never becomes dull. His punctuation is generally good. However, the student would have been better advised to use more shorter, snappier sentences. **11/15**

ACCURACY OF MECHANICS

There are a few spelling mistakes. **Marks: 4/5**

Total mark: 39/50 (B2)

9 Diary entries

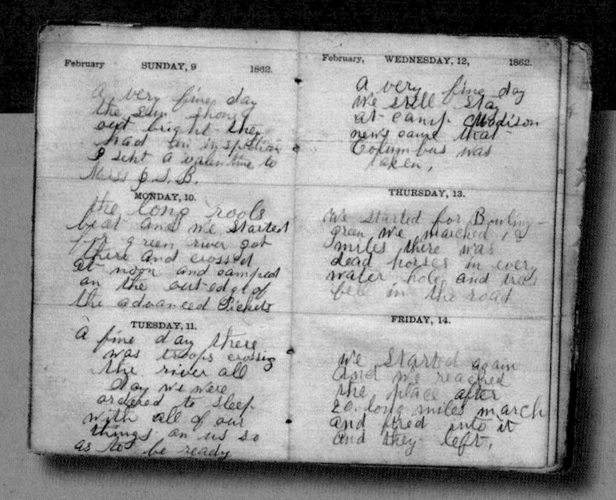

Diaries are a personal, private form of writing. They record thoughts, feelings and experiences.

CONTENT

As a rule of thumb, your diary entry should include the following features:

- The date
- A description of events that occurred on this date.
- Your reaction to these events

There are no hard-and-fast rules regarding tone in diary entries. Because they are not written for personal consumption, many diarists use an informal, chatty tone. However, some diarists use a serious, formal tone, even when describing their most intimate thoughts and experiences.

SAMPLE ANSWER 1

Write three or four diary entries that record the details of a disastrous holiday (real or imagined) that you experienced.

18 August

Dear Diary,
After waiting all summer for this 'wonderful' sun holiday, it seems Murphy's Law is proving itself once again. The weather couldn't be any worse than it is, and I think I am going to end up fighting with my friends if we have to stay indoors together any longer! Every little thing is beginning to annoy me and all I can do is shut myself away with you. Keep me sane! It's silly, but even Lorraine's coughing is rubbing me up the wrong way. But I can't say a word because, God knows, all the girls are in the same situation. I might just lie down for a while and see if the weather will let up later. ☹

19 August

Dear Diary,
So much for hoping the weather would get better. The weather forecast predicts gale force winds all day today and tomorrow, giving way to heavy rain for the rest of the week. Oh dear. Karen wanted to go outside anyway, but I didn't think it was a good idea, as chairs were almost flying around the pool outside! I couldn't blame her though; we're all suffering from cabin fever and going slightly crazy. Can this holiday get any worse?!

20 August

Dear Diary,
I spoke too soon yesterday and I think I dragged even more bad karma on our group. Karen ended up running outside after she nearly attacked Lorraine for coughing all the time (seems it annoyed everyone else as well, poor Lorraine). Unfortunately a slate fell off a roof due to the force of the wind and left Karen with a huge gash on her leg. The supervisor had to drive her to the hospital to get stitches. Seemingly it looked worse than it was, but I think everyone has given up on this horrible experience I shudder to call 'a holiday'. We've decided to get an early flight home tomorrow. The girls finally have some life in them. The idea of going home to home-cooked meals and meeting up with the rest of our friends is putting smiles on all out faces. Bon Voyage!

MARKS & COMMENTARY

CLARITY OF PURPOSE The student's answer is entirely relevant and focused. She has been asked to write three or four diary entries about a holiday gone wrong, and she has done just this. **15/15**

COHERENCE OF DELIVERY The informal register is perfect for a diary, and her references to the weather and her friends are ideal. The diary entries follow a logical progression, each day's entry following on from the previous and anticipating the next. **15/15**

EFFICIENCY OF LANGUAGE USE The student's vocabulary is good, and her sentence patterns varied and interesting. The diary entries are arranged nicely, and use lively and interesting phrasing that prevents them ever being dull. The use of the question mark followed by an exclamation mark at the close of the second entry is appropriate given the fact that this is written for a diary. **15/15**

ACCURACY OF MECHANICS The student's spelling and grammar are perfect. 5/5

Total mark: 50/50 (A1)

SAMPLE ANSWER 2

Write three of four diary entries by Jimmy, in which he describes his experience of Larry's visit to his house. (Note: This is an answer to a Question B that relates to the Frank O'Connor text in the Comprehension sample answer above.)

Friday 5th of May (morning)

Mam and Dad went away this weekend. Aunty May's sick again. Jesus if that woman could come down with any more illnesses she'll have no defences left in her.

Larry's coming over at five to keep me company til they come home on Monday. Larry and I don't really know how to cook so Mam left us with a chicken. I think we'll probably make sandwiches.

Friday 5th of May (evening)

Oh my God, I can't believe Larry brought his bear with him. You know at ten you think you'd be alright for a few nights without house comforts.

Larry's after bringing his trusty travel suitcase. I don't know what he put in it for his holidays this time but it took the two of us to pull it up the high flight of steps. We step one foot into the house and Larry just stares at the piano. I finally get him to move down the hall and he starts laughing at the toilet. I never really understood what was so funny.

It finally reached eight o'clock, we were both exhausted from playing cowboys and Indians we both nearly died in the bed as soon as we lay our heads down.

Saturday 6th of May

Larry was up at the crack of down peering though the binoculars watching everyone on their way to the market. The usual crowd you'd never really see on Larry's street, farmers, policemen and railwaymen.

After some breakfast we headed outside and rested against Crary's wall as the sun began to heat up. Some of the lads from Larry's lane came up chatting to us. When they were done talking about insubordinate, futile little matters we finally go to split into two teams for soccer.

We stuck Larry in Goal cause he always had this problem of touching the ball with his hands which in a way is very useful

We were in by seven bright because we got mass in the morning and we decided cause the night sky was so clear we'd bring the binoculars up to my room and look out over all of Dublin.

Running up to my room Larry in more of a sprinting mood beat me we sat at the biggest window. The sun was just setting. Lighting the whole area orange. We could see the whole road up and down. The Quarry was in view and at the end of it the tiny perked houses. Up to top were open field. You could see the gas lamps being turned on and starting to glow against the sky.

Larry just seemed to stare in astonishment that his home area could be so beautiful.

MARKS & COMMENTARY

CLARITY OF PURPOSE

The student has clearly read and understood the question. The student has been asked to write a series of diary entries describing Larry's visit from Jimmy's point of view. Everything she writes is relevant to, and focused on, the events described in the Frank O'Connor story. Her diary entries stay within the sphere of Larry's visit.

She shows that she understands what a diary entry is, and reproduces the conventions of the genre. **15/15**

COHERENCE OF DELIVERY

The student uses a register appropriate to the task and maintains it throughout the diary. She successfully manages to write as though she were Jimmy. The student displays a high level of creativity in her convincing and coherent portrayal of Larry's visit. **14/15**

EFFICIENCY OF LANGUAGE USE

This piece features some vibrant and lively use of language, which effectively conjures a fictional world. There is a decent level of vocabulary, and the sentence patterns are varied enough not to bore the reader.

The diary entries make good use of paragraphs, with each paragraph focusing on different aspects of Larry's visit. **13/15**

ACCURACY OF MECHANICS

There are several places where this piece departs from conventional grammar and syntax. However, this is excusable given the fact that the student is writing from Jimmy's point of view. In fact, these irregularities enhance our enjoyment of the piece. The spelling is accurate throughout. **5/5**

Total mark: 47/50 (A1)

FOCUS ON LANGUAGE STYLES

This piece of writing is a good example of the language of narration, telling the story of Larry's visit. To the author's credit, she effectively shapes the narrative, bringing the reader along with her. She also exhibits an understanding of how sentence structure should be varied in the language of narration.

10 Short talks

'The trouble with talking too fast is you may say something you haven't thought of yet.'
Ann Landers, newspaper columnist

'Before I speak, I have something important to say.'
Groucho Marx, comedic genius

PURPOSE OF THE SHORT TALK

As with all essays, it is vital that you remain highly conscious of what you are trying to do. Are you presenting an argument? Are you giving advice or information? Are you outlining your own thoughts and feelings on a given subject? As you plan and write your talk, remember that each paragraph should contribute to this goal. You will be penalised for straying off the point.

FORMAL SALUTATION When giving a short talk, it is best to begin with what is known as a 'formal salutation'.

- If you are addressing a formal gathering of people, you should begin your speech with the phrase 'Ladies and Gentlemen'.
- If there are dignitaries in your audience, you should include them in your salutation. For example, 'Mr President, ladies and gentlemen …'
- If you are addressing your classmates, you should open with 'My fellow classmates'.

TONE AND AUDIENCE Some Leaving Cert questions require you to adopt a serious tone. Others require you to adopt a more light-hearted tone. It is important that you practise writing both serious and light-hearted speeches.

Some Leaving Cert questions don't specify which tone you are to use in your speech. In these instances, you must decide which tone is most appropriate yourself. When doing this, it is important to be conscious of your audience. For example, a speech given to the UN about climate change should have a formal tone. On the other hand, if you are addressing your classmates, you may want to use a more relaxed, light-hearted tone.

Whatever tone you decide to use, make sure you maintain that tone throughout the speech.

WHO YOU ARE

Some speeches require you to imagine you are someone else. For example, you might be asked to imagine that you are a leading politician. It is important to imagine how you would speak as this character, and to maintain the appropriate tone and register throughout your speech.

PERSUASIVE SHORT TALKS

Some short talks in the Leaving Cert require you to convince your audience that something is the case. For example, you might be asked to convince your audience about the importance of human rights.

When writing such a short talk, you will need to use the language of argument, appealing to your audience's intellect through facts, logic and rational argument. You will also have to use the language of persuasion, appealing to your audience's emotions, prejudices and preconceived ideas.

In a persuasive short talk, you are trying to prove a point. Sometimes, you might want to state this point plainly in your opening paragraph. We see this in the following opening to a talk entitled 'Changing our lives to save our planet'.

Good evening Ladies and Gentlemen.

Man's impact on the environment over the course of the last century has been devastating. With unbridled consumption, economic growth, materialism, insensitive development and booming population growth, we have all but destroyed this great and beautiful planet. We have now come to a grave juncture, Ladies and Gentlemen, and the time for idle talk has passed. It is time for each of us to take responsibility for our actions and to change our lifestyles so that the environment can be saved. We are not helpless in this matter: there are many things we can start to do today that will help.

It is also possible to begin your speech with an 'impact' paragraph that grabs the audience's attention before stating your point clearly in the second paragraph. The 'impact' paragraph might often focus on a shocking statistic, real-life story or dramatic event that brings your point vividly to life. For example:

Ladies and Gentlemen, over forty per cent of all tropical forests have been destroyed, and another acre is lost each second. The annual catch in thirteen of the world's fifteen major fishing zones has declined. and in four of those – three in the Atlantic and one in the Pacific oceans – the catch has shrunk by a startling thirty per cent. One-half of our nation's lakes and one-third of our rivers are too polluted to be completely safe for swimming or fishing. Millions of pounds of toxic chemicals – like lead, mercury and pesticides – pour into our waterways each year, contaminating wildlife, seafood and drinking water.

I am here today to tell you what we can do to save our dying planet ...

Each paragraph you write should focus on a single topic. Each paragraph should support the point you make at the beginning of the talk.

In the body paragraphs of your talk, you can use facts and statistics to appeal to your audience's heads. You can also use real-life stories and emotional language to appeal to their hearts. Every single paragraph should be geared towards one thing: convincing the audience that your point of view is correct.

The closing paragraph should briefly summarise the main points of the talk before concluding with a snappy, memorable phrase. It can also be very effective to conclude your talk with a question that will linger in the audience's mind.

NON-PERSUASIVE SHORT TALK

Some short talks don't require you to persuade the audience that a particular point of view is correct. Instead, they invite you to explore your own thoughts and feelings on a given subject, or to talk about an experience you've had. For instance, you might be asked to talk about an interesting journey you've made or about the role sport plays in your life.

A non-persuasive short talk is not an excuse to write a rambling and incoherent piece. The essay still needs to be organised around a central point that you introduce in the opening paragraph. Each body paragraph should focus on a single topic and be related to this central point. The final paragraph should summarise the points made throughout the short talk, and end with a snappy, memorable statement.

SHORT TALK GIVING INFORMATION & ADVICE

You might also be asked to give a short talk that gives your audience information and advice. Such a talk will feature the language of information. In previous years, students were asked to give advice to first-year students in their school or to foreign students who have come to Ireland.

AN INFORMATIVE SHORT TALK SHOULD HAVE THE FOLLOWING FEATURES:

- An opening paragraph in which you introduce yourself and tell the audience what you are there to talk about.
- It should be concise. Each paragraph should be as short and as to the point as possible.
- It should be clear. Make each point as straightforward as possible. Remember, you are trying to help your audience, not confuse them further.
- It should be well crafted. Each paragraph should focus on a separate topic or piece of information.
- The final paragraph should summarise the points made throughout the short talk, and finish with a snappy, memorable statement.
- Don't stray off the point. Make sure that all the advice and information you give is relevant to the audience in question.

SAMPLE ANSWER 1

'The vulgar-fest that is much of modern Ireland'. Write a short talk in which you outline what you see as the main social problems affecting Ireland today.

Ladies and Gentlemen, thank you very much for taking the time to listen to this very important talk. I will be outlining the main social problems in the vulgar-fest that is much of modern Ireland.

1 As we are all aware Ireland today has a successful and wealthy economy thanks to the Celtic Tiger. As a nation we are a thriving, well-educated community, still rich in traditions and originality. However, despite these great fortunes we still have our faults. I am going to introduce you to a few of the social problems we are currently experiencing. I personally believe that informing the Irish public of these problems is the first step towards finding a solution.

divisions

This sentence is too long and loses coherence. The student would be better advised to use two or more short sentences here.

2 Although we are slow to admit it we are aware there are devisions between those who have money and those who have little of it. These social devisions can be seen by simply looking at the stereotypical view we have of those who live in Dublin four, or more commonly known as D4 compared to those living in the less advantaged areas of Dublin such as Ballymun. These social rifts may be a problem but it is only a very minor one. The bigger problems lie with the individuals.

3 The disadvantaged areas are experiencing many terrible problems: from minor ones such as binge drinking to the more worrying problems such as the use of hard drugs. Teenagers as young as twelve and thirteen are becoming hooked on these hard drugs with heroin being a major culprit. Usually children/teenagers begin to experiment with drugs either to get away from family abuse or because their parents are drug users already. Once they are hooked they cause more problems in the home – becoming violent or stealing from their family to pay for drugs. The problems grow bigger and the drugs become a form of escape. The more they take the drugs the bigger the problems grow. It is a vicious circle that spirals out of control and unfortunately is a common problem in disadvantaged areas.

4 On the other hand the slightly more advantaged areas are experiencing problems with personal competition to become better then everyone else. Bullying is a major problem with young people in Ireland because you have to fit a certain description to make friends. Those who have nice clothes, possibly a car, a nice house and the right look will fit in perfectly. Where does everyone else go? You become a social outcast if you don't wear the appropriate make-up, straighten/gel your hair or dress in the latest designer wear. The results of these strict unwritten rules of the school are horrifying. Suicide rates have increased and this is partially why.

5 By showing you a few social problems I hope that together we can come up with a solution to the problems or at least that everyone is aware of these problems and willing to try to put an end to them.

Thank you very much for your time and I hope it was worth your while.

MARKS & COMMENTARY

CLARITY OF PURPOSE

To the student's credit, she introduces a clear aim at the beginning of the talk: to outline modern Ireland's problems in the hope that publicly debating these issues will allow us to overcome them. Everything in the talk is relevant to, and focused on, this clear aim. Nothing irrelevant or distracting is introduced. The student succeeds in writing a short talk, reproducing the conventions of the genre, such as an opening salutation ('Ladies and Gentlemen)'. **14/15**

COHERENCE OF DELIVERY

The student uses what might be described as a semi-formal register appropriate to the task, and maintains it throughout the talk. However, the talk suffers from its lack of references and real-world examples. Though this is a short talk rather than a speech, perhaps a number of concrete examples and references could have been fitted in to reinforce the student's core point. The paragraphs flow nicely from each one to the next, with the topic sentence of each paragraph picking up on the closing sentence of the one before. However, the talk seems to lose coherence in paragraph 4, where this logical sequencing breaks down; in this paragraph, the student fails to focus on a single topic, instead flitting between a number of broadly-related issues. **8/15**

EFFICIENCY OF LANGUAGE USE

This talk has a reasonable level of vocabulary and varies the structure of its sentences enough to keep the reader involved. The student's phrasing however is at times a little dull, predictable and clichéd. With a little practise, the phrasing could be made livelier, fresher and more interesting. The student's use of paragraphs could also be improved. Paragraph 4, as we have noted, fails to focus on any particular topic, becoming somewhat rambling and incoherent. It could also be argued that the final two sentences of paragraph 2 should be placed at the beginning of paragraph 3, thereby creating two paragraphs that each focus on a distinct and particular topic. The student's use of syntax and punctuation is more than adequate, with the exception of one overly long and poorly constructed sentence. **10/15**

ACCURACY OF MECHANICS

The student's spelling and grammar are generally good, apart from the exceptions highlighted above. **4/5**

Total mark: 36/50 (B3)

FOCUS ON LANGUAGE STYLES

The student uses the language of information rather than the language of argument or the language of persuasion. Her stated aim is to inform her audience about evils in modern-day Ireland in the hope that learning about these evils might cause her audience to act. This talk features some good informative writing as she outlines social problems in a relatively clear and concise fashion. As an informative piece, however, this could be improved upon by the addition of examples, references and statistics.

SAMPLE ANSWER 2

Write a short talk in which you talk about the role of mobile phones and social-networking sites in young people's lives today.

poorly phrased

presumably the student means 'easily-influenced'

should be 'utensils'

Ladies and gerntlemen,

1 We have developed into a nation whose youth marvels at the modern day phenomenon of mobile phones and social-networking sites. These technical wonders capture and bewitch adolescents across the globe and have been incorporated into the neccessities of daily living. Such technologies are directly aimed at the most influential young people. It is thus no great surprise that it is this target audience who cannot imagine life without such utencils of modern day communication. They have become so supremely valuable to youngsters they are willing to dispense vast amounts of money on them each week, or allocate lengthy amounts of time to scavenging through the information readily available at the click of a mouse.

2 Why are mobile phones and social-networking sites so sacred to these young people? Because they offer more interaction with people than face-to-face talking can? Or because even if you're feeling down, you can mask your emotions and hide how you really feel about things or people? Or simply because its an easier, faster, more entertaining form of communication? All of the above. Adolescents have become netted into a web where modern-day technology can provide a more appealing form of communication.

3 We live in a hugely materialistic world where money really does make the world spin round. And mobile phone companies will create the most unique, up to date, utterly breathtaking piece of technology in order to spin our world faster. Of course, we no longer need to worry about carrying an iPod, a computer, a camera and a phone into town with us, we simply have a compact incorporation of the four essentials in life which can slip into a pocket. This will sort out all our problems. Or will it?

4 Many young people have evidently grown addicted to social-networking sites, such as Bebo, My Space and Facebook. These social havens remain home to vast amounts of material which can be entertaining for many younger people. It allows them to view photos, do quizzes, write comments and install videos. It is an appealing way to pass time, yet many youngsters are not aware of the vast bulk of valuable time they throw away sitting in front of computer screens. As a result of these websites proving so abundant and popular it is not suprising that they have eclipsed the technical-communication era into one so remarkably developed. Many feel they are vital in order to fit in, or can feel pressurised to open accounts to be socially accepted by groups.

This sentence is too long and poorly constructed, causing it to lose meaning and coherence.

This sentence is also somewhat clumsy, and could be better constructed.

5 It is tragic that these young people are growing so attached to this form of communication, that they forget how to conduct a verbal conversation without using slang. The abbreviations used in short-hand communication are so regularly used that they form part of the new English language. It must be admitted that these forms of correspondence are at times indispensable yet their over use in society is diminishing personal contact.

should be communication

6 I acknowledge the importance of mobile phones and social-networking sites in young people's lives today and that they do deliver a great extent of entertainment into their daily living. However, I urge young people who are in a sense addicted to these modern day communication phenomenons to use them sparingly. To conclude I would like to thank you for your attention during this talk. I hope you have found it both informative and beneficial and that I have heightened your awareness and understanding of the topic.

This is very poorly phrased.

should be 'phenomena'

CLARITY OF PURPOSE It must be admitted that the talk remains more or less focused on mobile phones and social-networking sites. Nothing irrelevant to this topic is introduced.

The student succeeds in writing a short talk, reproducing the conventions of the genre, such as an opening salutation ('Ladies and Gentlemen)'.

Unfortunately, however, the talk seems to lack a really clear and well-defined aim. While the student does indeed talk about these technologies, she might have profited by taking a definite stance on them and introducing it in the opening paragraph. Is she for or against these technologies? Is she here to point out dangers associated with them? By adopting such a definite take on these topics, she would have given her talk much more focus. **8/15**

COHERENCE OF DELIVERY The student uses what might be described as a semi-formal register appropriate to the task, and maintains it throughout the talk.

However, as is so often the case, the talk might have benefited from a couple of references or real-world examples. For example, the student might have referenced a survey or touched on an anecdote about Bebo-addiction.

There is a reasonable continuity of argument here, with each paragraph following more or less logically from the one before. Yet, there is also room for improvement in this area. With better planning. the argumentative 'flow' of the talk could be improved. **8/15**

EFFICIENCY OF LANGUAGE USE While the talk varies the structure of its sentences, several words are badly chosen or misused altogether, which lets the talk down badly.

There are several paragraphs where the student fails to focus on a single defined topic, instead flitting between a number of broadly related issues – for example, paragraphs 4 and 6.

The student's use of syntax and punctuation could also be improved as there are several overly long and poorly constructed sentences. **6/15**

ACCURACY OF MECHANICS As highlighted above, the student misspells several words. **2/5**

Total mark: 24/50 (D2)

SAMPLE ANSWER 3

We will now look at an answer from a different student to the same question.

Good afternoon, Ladies and Gentlemen, my name is Siobhan Hughes. Today I want to speak about the role of mobile phones and social-networking sites in young people's lives today.

Long, poorly constructed sentence. Should have been written as two shorter sentences.

Poor choice of word, – 'had' would have sufficed.

1. It is a relevant issue as it is frequently covered in the news headlines and forcing parents to consider what dangers their children are dwelling in. A dependency has been created within their lives, where constant visits to their second world must be obtained each day. Phone calls are almost that of an ancient matter as texting and posting comments on social-networking sites are dominating the communication methods of young people today. Not only can we access our friends profile pages where we can talk, see pictures and videos, we can also browse through strangers profiles and comb through their pages.

Long, poorly constructed sentence.

2. For what reason you may ask? Curiosity. If you like the look of someone and want to get to know them their Bebo or My Space profiles seem like the ideal situation. You can suss out their favourite hobbies, music, films and view what they are talking about with other online socialites. What we need to know is that there is NO privacy on these sites. People can read EVERYTHING that is contained within your profile page and their impression is what gives you your online status.

awkward sentence

3. I'm afraid to inform you that mobile phones and social-networking sites are in fact a huge factor in young people's lives today. If they don't have a mobile glued to their hand, they are immobilised in front of a computer screen. This phenomenon is gradually evolving beyond extremes! Bebo now advertised on TV – crazy as it sounds its true!, can now be accessed from mobile phones, giving us a constant usage to its site, creating an even larger fan base and an alarmingly dangerous addiction. Mobile Bebo2 is a scary thought, to think that wherever you may go, the cold impersonal internet relationships are following.

4. No one is ever quite sure whether being an internet socialite is a good or a bad thing! Personally, I enjoy the usage to keep in contact with far away friends and family. It is a good inexpensive method of communication, although once sucked into the deep addiction of almost living another life, it is difficult to escape.

Thank you for your time.

MARKS & COMMENTARY

CLARITY OF PURPOSE

The student has been asked to write a short talk about the role mobile phones and social-networking sites play in young people's lives today. Her answer shows that she has read and understood the question. Everything she writes is relevant to, and focused on, the task at hand.

However, the piece suffers from a lack of a clear aim. Though the student does tell the audience that she will be speaking about the role of social-networking sites in young people's lives, it is not until she nears the end of the talk that she makes her point of view clear.

She shows that she understands what a short talk is, and reproduces the conventions of the genre. She addresses her audience appropriately at the start: 'Ladies and Gentlemen'. She also addresses them throughout the talk, e.g. 'For what reason you may ask?' and 'I'm afraid to inform you ....' **11/15**

COHERENCE OF DELIVERY

The student uses a fairly informal register, and maintains this throughout the talk. Her references to 'Bebo' and 'My Space' are appropriate and well used. However, she could perhaps have sequenced her paragraphs better. For example, the opening of her third paragraph seems out of place, and might be better suited to the start of the talk. **11/15**

EFFICIENCY OF LANGUAGE USE

This piece features some vibrant and lively use of language, which serves to maintain the audience's interest and prevents the talk from becoming dull. The student engages the audience and effectively conveys the impression that she is in possession of information that they ought to hear, beginning one sentence with 'I'm afraid to inform you ...'

However, it could be argued that some of the third paragraph is melodramatic and out of keeping with the rest of the talk. Phrases such as 'evolving beyond control' and 'alarmingly dangerous addiction' seem to be a little over the top in the context of the material presented. **11/15**

ACCURACY OF MECHANICS

Though of a reasonable standard, the piece does feature some awkward phrases and poorly constructed sentences such as 'It is a relevant issue as it is frequently covered in the news headlines and forcing parents to consider what dangers their children are dwelling in'. The spelling is accurate throughout. **3/5**

Total mark: 36/50 (B3)

SAMPLE ANSWER 4

You have been asked to give a short talk on radio or television about a fundamental human right that you would like to see supported more strongly. Write out the text of the talk you would give.

Good evening ladies and gentlemen.

1. I urgently speak to you now in relation to a fundamental right, the fundamental right of a child to experience a childhood free of forced labour, which is, as we speak, being forsaken in lands abroad. The enslavement of children in furtherance of monetary gain is a critical blow against the rights of children everywhere. In areas like the Ivory Coast in Africa, cocoa farmers are luring children with promises of well-paid work, when in actual fact, they must work for nothing.

2. But why should the Irish people take heed? It is because, we the Irish, are perpetuating this atrocity through our ignorance of the true circumstances. And I hope that by the end of this speech, we as a nation will be more aware of what we buy, and under what conditions the products have been made.

3. Cocoa farmers instigate the slave trade, not with adults, but with children, too young to protect themselves. These children, ranging in ages from five to fifteen, are forced to work under horrible conditions, such as:

- being physically beaten for not carrying bags of beans twice their own weight
- being virtually starved
- being forced to live in festering hovels, which are rarely cleaned, with many other children.

We must be aware of the fact that buying certain chocolate products perpetuates these atrocities. By buying these products, we contribute to the pain these poor children experience, as it encourages farmers to continue working their 'slaves' to the bone.

should be circumvent

4. However there are ways to circumnavigate this problem. There are various charity services focused on aiding children in these circumstances. People can aid these children by helping to fund their education so they will not feel the need to work for next to nothing. Also, supporting FairTrade is beneficial in every regard, encouraging farmers in Third World countries to grow their produce and trade it fairly with the more developed countries. If we increase awareness of the products we are buying, and find out more about the circumstances in which the product is produced, less children will be in danger of being forced to work for nothing.

Thank you for your time.

MARKS & COMMENTARY

CLARITY OF PURPOSE The student succeeds in writing a short talk, reproducing the conventions of the genre, such as an opening salutation ('Good evening Ladies and Gentlemen)'.

The student begins by stating clearly what she intends to speak about: namely, the right that children have to a childhood free of labour. However, it could be argued that she gets sidetracked by her example of forced child labour in the cocoa industry, and that her speech is ultimately about this and not the abstract rights of children. **9/15**

COHERENCE OF DELIVERY The student uses a formal register appropriate to the task, and she maintains this throughout. Her paragraphs could, however, have been better sequenced. For example, paragraph 2 might have been more appropriately placed near the end of the talk. This would allow for the paragraph on the cocoa farmers to follow on from its introduction in the first paragraph. That said, the student does manage her paragraphs well, using each one to deal with a distinct point. As stated above, the example of the cocoa farmers dominates the essay, and ought to have been better managed. **11/15**

EFFICIENCY OF LANGUAGE USE The student displays a high level of vocabulary, and uses a variety of sentence patterns. She appeals to the audience on a number of occasions, and uses persuasive language appropriate to the task. Her punctuation and syntax are of a good standard. **13/15**

ACCURACY OF MECHANICS Spelling and grammar are of a very high standard throughout. **5/5**

Total mark: 38/50 (B2)

11 Magazine & newspaper articles

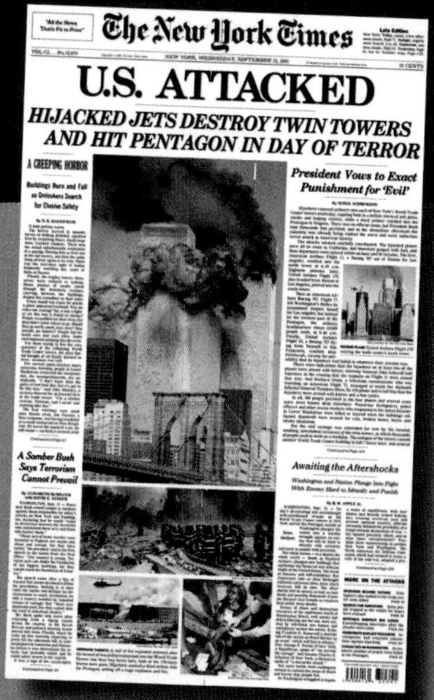
The New York Times

U.S. ATTACKED

HIJACKED JETS DESTROY TWIN TOWERS AND HIT PENTAGON IN DAY OF TERROR

A CREEPING HORROR

President Vows to Exact Punishment for 'Evil'

A Somber Bush Says Terrorism Cannot Prevail

Awaiting the Aftershocks

Magazine and newspaper articles offer the writer's take on the world.

INTRODUCTION

When writing an article, it is important to be aware of the following:

HEADLINE, BYLINE AND SUBHEADING A headline is the title of the piece. It should state clearly what the article is about. Light or humorous articles often use quirky or funny headlines to catch the reader's attention. This is less common in serious articles.

A byline is the author's name, which occurs just under the headline.

A subheading provides a short sentence under the headline that sums up the central thrust of the article.

TONE Some Leaving Cert questions require you to adopt a serious tone. Others require you to adopt a more light-hearted tone. It is important that you practise writing both serious and light-hearted articles.

Some Leaving Cert questions don't specify which tone you are to use in your article. In these instances, you must decide which tone is most appropriate yourself. When doing this, it is important to be conscious of the topic you are addressing; for example, if you are writing an article about the plight of people society has rejected, it might be advisable to adopt a serious tone. On the other hand, if you are exploring aspects of your own family life, you might wish to adopt a more relaxed, light-hearted tone.

Whatever tone you decide to use, make sure you maintain that tone throughout the article.

Some articles use flair, wit and humour. For example, the opening paragraph of this article on the stresses of modern living uses all three to make its point:

> We all know the feeling. It's seven o'clock on a Wednesday evening, and while the rest of the working world is settling down to their nightly fix of soap operas and junk TV, you're having a staring match with a school or college project that was due in yesterday. On top of this, your parents or flatmates (delete as appropriate) have decided that it's your turn to unblock the septic tank; while your boss has been on the phone haranguing you to do 'just' four hours while he thinks up new and exciting ways to rip off the consumer. And let's not forget answering the twenty texts an hour from your friends telling you how hard their life is. There's no doubt about it: modern life is stressful, and the younger you are the more stressful it is. Short of writing a strongly-worded letter to God, there's probably no way of eliminating all the stress in your life, but by taking the following advice, you might hopefully avoid at least some of the more common forms of it. Considering that the alternative is to die of a heart attack at twenty-six, it's definitely worth giving it a go.

Some serious articles, like the following, maintain a serious, formal tone throughout.

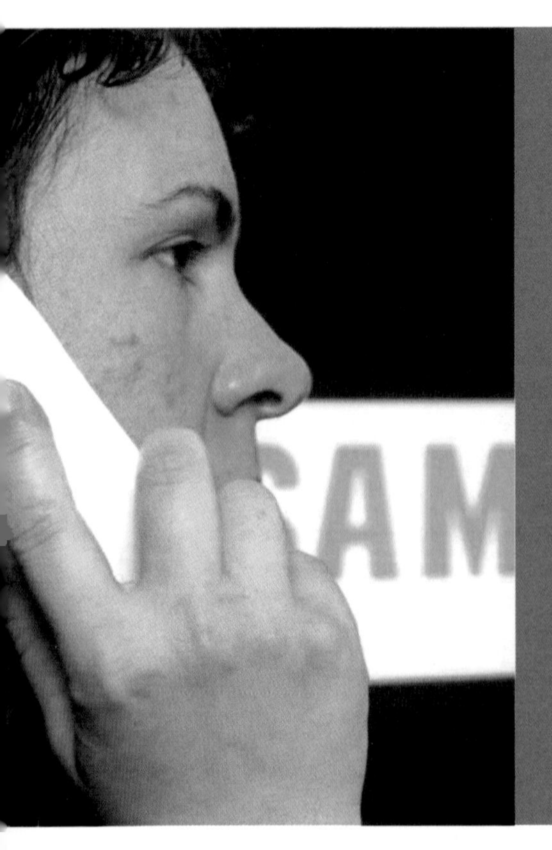

> Like me, you're young; and like me, you probably know at least one person who has had a mental breakdown, harmed themselves or committed suicide in response to the pressures of modern living. While being young has probably always been a stressful experience, there can be no doubt that living in contemporary Ireland places demands on young people that are difficult, if not impossible, to meet. Last year alone, more young people died from suicide than any other single cause, and this statistic does not even factor in the huge incidence of self-harm among people below the age of twenty-five. Though the government is slowly waking up to the scale of this problem, its sluggish response only goes to show that it doesn't fundamentally care about the problems faced by young people in modern Ireland. In view of the failure of 'official' Ireland to offer any worthwhile advice on the topic of stress, my goal here is to explore how young people might combat some of the more common pressures they encounter in modern life. Necessarily, my advice will only reflect my personal experiences, and is in no way meant to substitute for professional opinion; but I've found the following things useful in dealing with stress, and hopefully, you might too.

However, it is also possible to write a serious article that uses some wit and humour without lapsing into a chatty, informal tone.

It cannot be stressed enough here that the best way of gaining an insight into how to write articles is to read them. Indeed, if you encounter an article writer that you particularly like, there is no harm in trying to copy the style and layout of their articles. As Oscar Wilde observed, imitation is the sincerest form of flattery.

PERSUASIVE ARTICLES

In some articles you are trying to prove a point, to convince your readers that your take on the given topic is correct. Sometimes, you might want to state this point plainly in your opening paragraph. We see this in the following opening:

> **It is cliché, not plagiarism, that is the problem with our stilted, room-temperature political discourse. It used to be that thinking people would say, with at least a shred of pride, that their own convictions would not shrink to fit on a label or on a bumper sticker. But now it seems that the more vapid and vacuous the logo, the more charm (or should that be 'charisma'?) it exerts. Take 'Yes We Can,' for example. It's the sort of thing parents might chant encouragingly to a child slow on the potty-training uptake.**

It is also possible to begin your article with an 'impact' paragraph that grabs the reader's attention, before stating your point clearly in the second paragraph. The 'impact' paragraph might often focus on a shocking statistic, real-life story or dramatic event that brings your point vividly to life.

Each paragraph should focus on a single topic. Each paragraph should support the point you make at the beginning of the article.

In the body paragraphs of your article, you can use facts and statistics to appeal to your audience's heads. You can also use real-life stories and emotional language to appeal to their hearts. Every single paragraph should be geared towards one thing: convincing the audience that your point of view is correct.

The closing paragraph should briefly summarise the main points of the article, before concluding with a snappy, memorable phrase. It can also be very effective to conclude your article with a question that will linger in the audience's mind.

NON-PERSUASIVE ARTICLES

Some articles don't require you to persuade the reader that a particular point of view is correct. Instead, they invite you to explore your own thoughts and feelings on a given subject. In previous years, students have been asked to explore the aspects of their families that are special to them, or the role music plays in their lives.

A non-persuasive article is not an excuse to write a rambling and incoherent essay. The article still needs to be organised around a central point that you introduce in the opening paragraph. Each body paragraph should focus on a single topic and be related to this central point. The final paragraph should summarise the points made throughout the article, and finish with a snappy, memorable statement.

SAMPLE ANSWER 1

'Celebrities can inspire people of all ages to be better than they are.' Write an article for a serious newspaper or journal about today's celebrity culture.

The Age of the Celebrity

1. If you are in a serious accident the only person you should call for help is your local Scientologist. This was Tom Cruise's advice during one of his interviews and undoubtedly this statement has swayed many Cruise fans. Celebrities can inspire people of all ages but is it always for the better? It is beyond me what a Scientologist can do to help that an ambulance, a doctor or close family member can't.

2. You only have to look as far as your local newsagent to witness the deep interest people have with celebrities. Shops are filled with glossy magazines and tabloid newspapers displaying the latest scandals in the lives of the celebrities. Why do people feel they need to know about the latest pandemonia caused by Britney Spears or hear the latest juicy details about the marriage of Posh and Becks. These stories have no real effect on our lives yet we care about these matters. Some care so deeply they strive to be more and more like the celebrities they see in magazines and on television. Their style and look is cloned. Their dieting regime and hobbies are copied. Is this simply a pathetic attempt to feel important and admired by others?

3. We are all aware of the hype surrounded by the reality television show Big Brother. The latest antics of the contestants are splashed across newspapers and magazines daily. These contestants are a perfect example of the desperate attempts people will make to experience life in the limelight. They are obviously aware they have no real talent and will grasp any opportunity to be seen by the public. The life of former Big Brother contestant Jade Goody, known for her shocking and vulgar behaviour, is still under the constant and watchful eye of the public. Her actions which caused uproar, unfortunately for those of us who are not fans of reality television and celebrity scandals, allowed her to stretch her fifteen minutes of fame into years. These are the 'celebrities' who are having a negative impact on our society. Fame should be reserved for the hard working role models of our world not the desperate, talentless, attention seeking celebrities who still seem to be inspiring people to be like them!

4. Despite this some of the lazy, talentless celebrities have inspired people to take the wrong path in life. I recently watched a television programme 'I want my daughter to be like Jordan', which disgusted me. The mother of a nine-year-old girl was encouraging her daughter to dress skimpy and act a little slutty. The innocent child was lying on the bed in her underwear while her mother took photos. She indulged us in the fact she should be getting her daughter breast implants and any other cosmetic surgery necessary. Jordan has recently cleaned up her act but the image of her falling out of nightclubs and bars and baring all still remains. Is this what our society has come to? The inspiration of celebrities has caused nine-year-old girls to forget their dreams of growing up to be ballerina or fairy princess and replaced them with desires to be a page three girl.

5. People like the mother of this child should be locked up with the rest of the celebrity fanatics that pose a threat to our society thanks to their 'great inspiration'.

MARKS & COMMENTARY

CLARITY OF PURPOSE

The student has been asked to write a serious newspaper article. She clearly understands what a newspaper article is, and is capable of writing in a style that is appropriate to one. However, certain words and phrases used (e.g. 'slutty') are inappropriate to a *serious* article, and belong more to a light-hearted or tabloid article.

All the material presented here is relevant to the task that the student has been given. However, the material has been organised in a way that lacks focus. The writer fails to outline a clear aim for her essay early on. It is only at the end of paragraph 3, which is the second-last full paragraph, that the writer introduces her own take on celebrity culture. **17/30**

COHERENCY OF DELIVERY

The writer adopts a chatty, informal tone, which she successfully maintains throughout. As we have noted, however, the tone and register are slightly less formal than required by the set task. The writer makes excellent use of references and examples, which serve to persuade the reader that her complaints about celebrity culture are justified. For example, her reference to the programme 'I want my daughter to be like Jordan' successfully provokes the reader's outrage and disbelief when it comes to celebrity culture.

There is a reasonable level of continuity of argument in this essay. Each paragraph focuses on the writer's central theme and logically connects to the paragraph that came before it. However, this argument could be sequenced and managed much more effectively. The student might have been better advised to state her point of view in a very clear way at the beginning of the essay and arrange the remaining paragraphs so that they clearly support this point of view. **22/30**

EFFICIENCY OF LANGUAGE USE

This essay is written in a lively, interesting fashion. The opening paragraph, in particular, catches the attention of the reader. There is a good level of vocabulary and a good variance of sentence patterns. In particular, each paragraph opens in a different fashion, which avoids the essay becoming monotonous. The essay is well paragraphed, with each paragraph focusing on one topic. In terms of syntax, the writer makes very few errors, but, like many students, she has several sentences that are too long and confuse the reader, e.g. 'Fame should be reserved for the hard working role models of our world not the desperate, talentless, attention seeking celebrities who still seem to be inspiring people to be like them!' **25/30**

ACCURACY OF MECHANICS

Apart from the few mistakes highlighted above, the student displays a good knowledge of spelling and grammar. **8/10**

Total mark: 72/100 (B3)

SAMPLE ANSWER 2 SAME TOPIC, DIFFERENT STUDENT

Playing the Fame Game

1. In modern society it is difficult to escape the constant influence of the celebrity world. Everywhere we go we are persistently being bombarded with images, reports and accounts of various celebrities and their scandalous and glamorous lives. We can see and hear about these people at the touch of a button as this information is available on the television, radio and the internet as well as in newspapers and magazines. Indeed it is often the case that we know more about the life and experiences of a celebrity than we do about our own next-door neighbour.

2. Many people today would quickly admit that celebrity culture is an important aspect of their life, as more and more people buy several 'gossip' magazines every week in an effort to escape from the realities of their lives or as an outlet for their imaginations. An increasing amount of people earn their living from celebrity culture. For example the paparazzi, talent agents and the creators of television shows. To these people, the development and progress of the celebrity world is an extremely important element of their own life. But how does the increasing influence of the celebrities in our world affect the lives of the rest of us?

3. The children and teenagers of this generation are growing up continuously exposed to celebrities. It is quite obvious that this vulnerability and exposure can have a dramatic influence on their behaviour. Children today are becoming increasingly 'mature' for their age as exposure to the celebrity culture of sex, drugs and glamour is taking its toll on their lives. A recent survey conducted in Irish secondary schools found that fifty-one per cent of fifteen year olds admitted to being drunk at some stage and forty-seven per cent of eighteen year olds have experimented with drugs, a figure which rises substantially when these young people reach third level education.

4. In recent weeks the world has watched in horror as the scandals involving the pop stars Britney Spears and Amy Winehouse have unfolded before our eyes. It is obvious from the interest in these women that the world of celebrity culture is increasingly important in our lives. Many ordinary people care a great deal about the welfare of these women and have an interest in their well-being.

5. However, despite the negative influence of celebrity culture and its incredible grip on our society, one may forget the positive aspects of the celebrity world, which continue to make an important contribution to our lives and the lives of many world wide. It is important not to forget the beneficial and powerful work being done by celebrities such as Bono and Bob Geldof in their efforts to improve the world in which we live. These famous people have used their positions of influence, power and wealth to manifest positive changers in the lives of less fortunate people.

6. Celebrities like these have founded or supported charitable organisations, continue to make the position of the celebrity an important and necessary one in our society. Nevertheless, the shameful aspects of celebrity life sometimes overshadow the hard work and dedication of other celebrities.

7. The value of celebrity among ordinary people is high in our world today and every day more and more people dream of achieving the same position of fame and fascination as the celebrities they see so often through the media. It is true to say that many of the celebrities we see every day are 'famous for being famous'. The majority of people do not know the reasons behind their fame. Such celebrities may have achieved their popularity through reality television shows. Many a fading celebrity has attempted to regain his or her position and recognition through television programmes such as 'I'm a Celebrity Get Me Out of Here' and 'Celebrity Big Brother'.

8. It is obvious from the popularity of programmes such as these that celebrity culture is important and is very much a desired aspiration for many people. Year after year, thousands of hopefuls audition for a place on 'Big Brother' or exhibit their musical abilities and talents on 'The X-Factor'. These people long for the fame and wealth, which celebrity life offers to those willing and able to take on its demands.

9. Although it is clear that celebrity culture is woven into our society and is an integral part of the lives of many people, it is important that we learn to distance ourselves from its influence. Of course it is entertaining to enjoy gossiping about the dramatic lives of celebrities we see, but we must remind ourselves that these celebrities are people, not unlike ourselves. Although the celebrity world is a significant and powerful part of modern culture and entertainment, it should not control or affect our lives to the extent that it changes how we feel about ourselves as individuals. And so, in conclusion, it is essential to accept our own characters, strengths and weaknesses and not be persuaded by the sometimes disreputable lives of the celebrities we see.

MARKS & COMMENTARY

CLARITY OF PURPOSE

This student displays a good understanding of what a serious article entails, and uses a tone appropriate to such a piece of writing. She writes in a reasonably formal and serious style, and avoids slipping into a more chatty register.

The essay is focused *on* and relevant *to* the set task, with each paragraph falling within the scope of the essay title. However, it could be argued the essay lacks a clear aim. The student's personal viewpoint on the matter is not clearly stated at the start of the essay, which makes it unclear what message she is ultimately trying to put across. Her viewpoint only becomes clear in the final paragraph. **25/30**

COHERENCY OF DELIVERY

As we have noted, the student adopts a suitable tone and register that she maintains throughout the article.

The writer makes good use of references and examples, referring to relevant television programmes, statistics and particular celebrities. The writer introduces many different ideas, but remains focused on the essay topic. For example, she introduces Bob Geldof, but doesn't then launch into a long discussion of Live Aid, instead remaining focused on the set task.

This essay exhibits a high level of continuity of argument. Each paragraph is relevant to celebrity culture, and for the most part the paragraphs follow on from one another in a logical fashion.

To some extent, the article is let down by its sequencing. The student makes a lot of interesting points, but could have arranged them in a more coherent fashion. For instance, she might have been better advised to place paragraphs 7 and 8 after paragraph 2, as paragraphs 2, 7, 8 and 3 all deal with the attention celebrities receive in today's world. As it is, the essay jumps around too much in its final paragraphs. **25/30**

EFFICIENCY OF LANGUAGE USE

The student makes no real errors with punctuation or syntax, and also paragraphs very well, with each paragraph focusing on a particular topic. The article reads extremely well, starting each paragraph differently, and with some lively and interesting phrasing using a broad vocabulary. **28/30**

ACCURACY OF MECHANICS

The student displays an excellent knowledge of spelling and grammar. **10/10**

Total mark: 88/100 (A2)

12 Personal essays

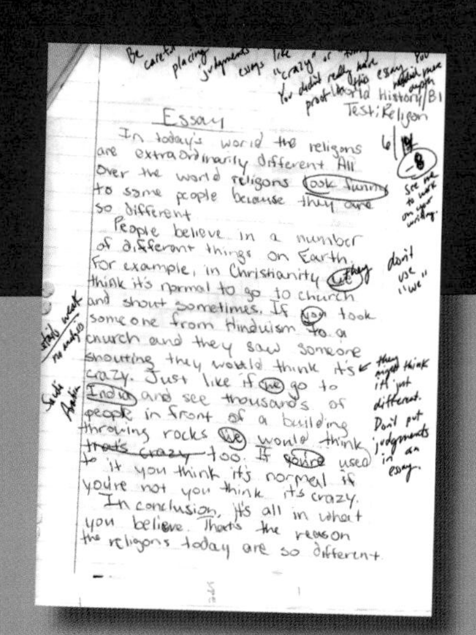

A personal essay has been defined as an essay written without any specific publication in mind.

INTRODUCTION

TONE

Some Leaving Cert questions require you to adopt a serious tone. Others require you to adopt a more light-hearted tone. It is important that you practise writing both serious and light-hearted essays.

Some Leaving Cert questions don't specify which tone you are to use in your essay. In these instances, you must decide which tone is most appropriate yourself. When doing this, it is important to be conscious of the topic you are addressing.

As always, whichever tone you decide to use, make sure you maintain that tone throughout the essay.

PERSUASIVE PERSONAL ESSAYS

In some essays, you are trying to prove a point – to convince your readers that your take on the given topic is correct. For instance, students have been asked to give their take on recent world events, and on the ideals and passions of youth.

Sometimes, you might want to state your point of view plainly in the opening paragraph. It is also possible to begin your essay with an 'impact' paragraph that grabs the reader's attention before stating your point clearly in the second paragraph. The 'impact' paragraph might often focus on a shocking statistic, real-life story or dramatic event that brings your point vividly to life.

Each body paragraph should focus on a single topic and support the point you make at the beginning of the essay.

In the body paragraphs of your essay, you can use the language of argument and the language of persuasion. Use facts and statistics to appeal to your readers' heads. You can also use real-life stories and emotional language to appeal to their hearts. Every single paragraph should be geared towards one thing: convincing the reader that your point of view is correct.

The closing paragraph should briefly summarise the main points of the essay before concluding with a snappy, memorable phrase. It can also be very effective to conclude your speech with a question that will linger in the reader's mind.

NON-PERSUASIVE PERSONAL ESSAYS

Some personal essays don't require you to persuade the reader that a particular point of view is correct. Instead, they invite you to explore your own thoughts and feelings on a given subject. In previous years, students have been asked to explore their sense of what it means to be Irish or to recount their childhood memories.

A non-persuasive essay is not an excuse to write a rambling and incoherent piece. The essay still needs to be organised around a central point that you introduce in the opening paragraph. Each body paragraph should focus on a single topic and be related to this central point. The final paragraph should summarise the points made throughout the essay, and finish with a snappy, memorable statement.

SAMPLE ANSWER 1

Write a personal essay in which you explore your sense of what it means to be Irish.

You'll often stop and wonder what does it mean to be Irish. The majority of the time you won't have a clue but in one of these rare moments of brilliance it will hit you. You'll sit back and gaze in awe as the answer unfolds in front of you like a movie. As if someone's gotten into your mind and picked out the very core of your masterpiece. This very same thing happened to myself once. It felt as if I was watching in on a fifty six inch wide screen television with every little details picked up on. Deuce the lights, cue the surround sound, take a seat and travel back to a life time of Irish greatness that made us what we are today. An island of nations. Twentieth Century Fox intro starts to play. The trailers of the up and coming movies finish. The age limit of the movie with whose starring pops up. Actors unknown but the age limit seems to be over eighteen. A Narrator over head of my voice starts to play, reading a script of which it means to be Irish from my point of view. Is it something your born into? Is it something you feel? Is it something you acquire? Really I think it's all of the above.

A somewhat odd sentence; not sure that it works.

Poorly constructed sentence.

Douse?

Too many short and poorly constructed sentences used here; the effect is rather annoying.

what

An aerial view of Ireland comes into view. Quickly zooms into nineteen fifty's Dublin. A suburban pub. A glimpse of where Ireland's drinking problems readily began. The binge drinking that would haunt us still to this day. A boy of sixteen would be taken into the pub for his first pint. This was believed to make him a man and a true Irish man.

incomplete sentence

This is still the case of today where every Irish person believes the only way they are full pledged Irish is by drinking. The little voice crops up again. Your not born with the knowledge you're destined to drink yourself into adulthood. You do not feel it growing up, it's not in your veins. This is something that is acquired and required of you by your fathers, grandfathers, brothers and friends. So this has got to be the very last thing that makes your Irish.

fully

You're

The old ceili, the land of music and dance. Although this has died out it plays a great role in how we get where we are today. Boys are on one side and girls on the other. Reared up and exhilarated to as soon as the music starts. One tap, two taps, three taps of the spoons, The Bank blast into full swing. The fiddler moving his arm up and down at sprinter's pace. The boys playing the tin. The man on the old squeeze box blasting out the tunes. God how the crack was mighty. Mind you we only made it til about half ten because everybody was ready to pass out with exhaustion. This is not something your born with though oh no, this is something you feel. The beat of the music running through your veins. Longing to escape and release itself among the world.

incomplete sentence

craic

sentence fragment

continued over

continued from previous page

SAMPLE ANSWER 1

poorly written

badly phrased

unusual word selection

poor choice of expression

again badly phrased

The student uses the device of the narrator in an inconsistent and confusing manner.

The student is losing focus here and not managing her ideas well.

Culture has changed over the years but something new has entered into Ireland's society today and is a hugely debated and topical issue is sex. Both male and female, young and old are entering more and a more into one night stand relationships. More and more people are perceiving this as I'm Irish now. If this epidemic continues people are going to forget what it really means to be Irish. We as an Irish society are now taking things at face value. The 'kiss me I'm Irish' t-shirts and 'F@CK me I'm Irish' t-shirts are provoking this concept more and more nowadays, especially on the younger people of today's social status. In my opinion this is totally wrong. This has nothing to do with being Irish. This little narrator pops up in a puff of smoke. This has got to be the worst reason anybody in the history of Ireland has every come up with of what it means to be Irish. Having sex for the sake of having sex is totally unacceptable and is more often then not pressurises onto us. It is also just a money making scheme by company's to sell their products. This is not Irish this is a national problem that needs to be sorted.

Poorly constructed sentence with bad grammar.

confusing, difficult to grasp

The hurley and sloitar were placed in our hands many years ago and it was one of the first things that gave us a sense of what is to be Irish. It made up proud. Our sporting talents is not what it means in my opinion to be Irish though. Through the years Ireland has made many a great sporting career for young men and women. The Old games of Gaelic society are starting to catch on with some other parts of the world now though. Gaelic football and hurling are two of the greatest games an Irish person can undertake. The skills involved is the speed, the precision, each time a player sets foot out on the pitch. A distant voice begins to seep back though the privilege and pride we feel when you play for your club, town, county and country is an unreal sense of a small part of which it means to be Irish.

having the ability to converse

odd, poor sentence

eccentric

syntax

The most definite answer I could give of what it means to me to be Irish though is speech and conversation. The people's people we are. We have no boundaries, no limits when it comes to speaking to other people. It doesn't matter if we know them or not. Some people think we are a bit excentric for coming up to them and starting a random conversation. We are the most friendly people on this planet of earth in my opinion. We have no fear of making new friends and meeting new people. Seeking new connections globally through people. 'This being this is Ireland. This is exploration. This is life.

'Welcome to Ireland, Welcome to Irish Life. Welcome to the sense of being a people person a person of all the world. After all we are an island of Nations.'

MARKS & COMMENTARY

CLARITY OF PURPOSE

The student has been asked to explore her sense of what it means to be Irish. However, much of her answer is somewhat irrelevant to the task she has been set. While she identifies several features of Irish life – for example, drinking, Gaelic games and Irish music – her discussion of these topics seems unconnected to her own sense of Irishness.

It is only late in the essay that the student finally reveals to us what she regards as the essence of Irishness: talking and conversation. To an extent, therefore, the essay loses focus. The student is not helped by the fact that she fails to establish a clear aim or viewpoint early in the essay. **15/30**

COHERENCY OF DELIVERY

The essay suffers from a lack of continuity in its argument. The student makes several valid points about Irish life, and uses some relevant examples and references, but she fails to arrange the paragraphs to form a coherent argument.

The essay has a reasonable flow but the device that the student has chosen to use – being in a cinema and observing a film that portrays various aspects of Irish society – is not properly developed. At moments throughout the essay, she seems to have forgotten about this device completely. Eventually, it seems to only interfere with her train of thought and the logic of her argument.

The essay is written in an informal, chatty, whimsical tone, with the student adopting an amused and amusing take on Irish life. This is maintained throughout. **14/30**

EFFICIENCY OF LANGUAGE USE

This is a poorly written piece at times, though it does, to its credit, feature some lively and interesting phrasing, e.g., 'One tap, two taps, three taps off the spoons, The Band blasts into full swing. The fiddler moving his arm up and down at sprinter's pace'. There is also a reasonable level of vocabulary and a good variety of sentence patterns.

From a more technical standpoint, the essay is split into well-defined paragraphs, each dealing with a distinct topic. However, the sentences are often badly constructed, and the reader has to work hard to make sense of what is happening at times. The student's rather informal and creative approach to the subject is to be welcomed, but it does not give her a licence to ignore punctuation and proper sentence structure. **13/30**

ACCURACY OF MECHANICS

There are numerous instances of bad spelling and grammar. **4/10**

Total mark: 46/100 (D)

SAMPLE ANSWER 2

'Every now and again I can remember something of the gay garden that was childhood's.' Write a personal essay in which you explore some of your earliest childhood memories.

length of sentence

1. Although many of my friends claim to have no memory of it, I can vividly recall the first morning I went to school. At nursery and pre-school, I think I was dimly aware that at some point down the line, I would be going to a big building somewhere wearing a coloured jumper and shirt with a bag of books on my back and having to stay there for a good part of the day until I was let go home again to play and watch television. I remember pre-school being fun: a couple of hours paying different games and looking through books that sometimes seemed to be telling interesting stories. I was reliably informed by a cousin, though, that school itself was not going to be any fun at all.

2. I have a vague memory of being fitted with the school uniform and liking the green jumper with the gold crest, although I definitely did not like the black shoes that were part of the package. Choosing a schoolbag was exciting, and I think I selected a blue and yellow number that I definitely thought was very eye-catching and colourful.

3. On the morning itself, I woke up with a sense of excitement, although not without a few nerves, as I had no idea what to expect. My mother drove us to the school, and she was full of encouraging words about the new friends I would make and the fun I would have. I couldn't think why she would lie to me, so I tried to put my reservations aside and did my best to believe her.

4. On arriving at the school gate, however, I had my first doubts. There were what seemed to be hundreds of boys my own age milling about with their mothers, and as far as I could make out, quite a large percentage were crying and demanding to be let go home with mammy. I began to wonder what it was that I had let myself in for. What did these people know that I did not? Obviously, it was something terrible. I remember looking up at my mother seeking reassurance and receiving a comforting pat on the head in return. She told me that those boys were only being big babies and that I would soon see that everything was alright. She couldn't wait to pick me up later so I could tell her all about it. I believed her, although when I saw her walk off and start daubing her eyes with a tissue, I was a bit dubious. I then walked gamely into the school hall, waiting for what would come. After that, I recall no more of that day, so either it was nothing too terrible, or else I have buried it as being too much of a trauma to recall!

5. One of my most vivid memories from early childhood is that of watching the large food market in town being burnt almost to a shell one summer's day. The fire began at ten o' clock that morning and news of it spread quickly around the city. Apparently, the fire-brigade were having great difficulty in containing the blaze and it was reckoned that the building had no chance of survival. My father thought this was too good a spectacle to miss, so he summoned me from the back garden for a walk up town to witness the drama.

6. There is something about fire that people find particularly compelling. Maybe it connects with the juvenile instinct to wreak havoc and destroy everything in sight in some sort of world-size tantrum, but the spectacle of red flames licking an object or a building to ashes mesmerises most of us. When I was a young child, the sight of a blaze was particularly hypnotic. What our father brought to see was like having a spectator's view of hell. The main entrance to the market was a large archway with a black ornate gate that looked almost medieval in its design. A large crowd had gathered as close to the entrance as they could and were eagerly peering into the halls inside. At this point the flames were still largely in the back of the building but were rapidly spreading outward, and the acidic stench of smoke was starting to fill the air.

us?

7. My father took us as close to the gate as safety would allow (the bulk of the fire fighters must have been at the back entrance) and put me on his shoulders to get a better view of the drama inside. The sight of flames licking the ceiling and gradually heading toward the front entrance was both compelling and terrifying. This was pure destruction, of the kind we saw in our comic-books and movies and had never dreamed of witnessing in the reality of our sheltered lives.

8. Although our parents and teachers had been careful enough not to introduce us to the concept of hell in any real detailed way yet, we had at school gained some idea of what it was meant to signify. The general consensus was that it involved being burnt alive forever in some enormous pit while being prodded and poked relentlessly by devils with permanently fixed evil grins. As children, we were unsure as to the truth of these rumours. Places like Heaven, Narnia and Middle-Earth were appealing places that one occasionally daydreamed of. Hell was only a bad dream, a thought that flickered occasionally across the mind. But now in front of me was a sneak preview of that terrible place. The sight of such an inferno on the main street was shocking enough. What, therefore, could this place under the ground that all of the bad people were going to be in forever hold in terms of flames and torment? It was enough to set me thinking for a while, and to make sure that my nightly conversations with God were a bit longer and more involved than usual.

9. One of childhood's biggest adventures that still remains fresh and powerful in my mind is my first family trip to London, or rather the flight that got us there. Planes fascinate most young boys and I was no exception to the rule. Whenever I was at the airport with my parents to either collect or see someone off, I would stand rapt at the window of the upper lounge, watching with great excitement the planes taxi for take-off or come in to land. The question of how the planes got off the ground was one that did not seem open to an easy explanation, and it always seemed like a minor miracle when the tip of an aircraft would nose its way into the air and seemingly drag the rest of itself almost reluctantly into the sky. How did this happen? Speed was obviously important, but then again, I had seen cars tearing along the streets and remain determinedly earth-bound. Clearly then, it all had to do with the wings. But how? Birds tended to flap theirs, as far as I could make out, to get themselves airborne, whereas the wings of planes did not seem to move at all. When I was told one day by my mother toward the end of senior infants that we were going to London in early July for a holiday, I was practically quivering with excitement, not only at the thought of seeing a big city that I had heard mentioned on television a good deal, but also of the magical prospect of being in a plane and flying through the sky.

my

in need of punctuation

Be careful with long sentences

10. The first priority on the day was to ensure I got a window seat. Although technically I was suppose to be on the aisle, my father was kind enough to allow me the privilege of the inside seat that would allow me to survey the land and seas below. Although I was hugely excited at the prospect of flying and being in a foreign city, I was also a little nervous. I knew planes crashed occasionally, but I thought I would have had to be highly unlucky if my first flight was earmarked for disaster. Nevertheless, I craned over the seat to watch the airhostess demonstrate how to fasten our seatbelts and what to do if the worst came to the worst. I distinctly remember being disappointed, and a little puzzled, as to why there were no parachutes under our seats. On the other hand, it was also a sign that the chances of anything going wrong were surely very small.

continued over

continued from previous page

SAMPLE ANSWER 2

11. Once we strapped in and ready to go, all I could think of was the take-off. One of my nastier schoolmates, upon learning of my good luck in heading to London in only the second week of the summer holidays, had been generous enough to inform me that the most dangerous parts of flying were taking off and landing. This, he said in the obvious hope of seeing my face drop and going ghastly pale, was when disaster struck. I remember thinking that this wasn't too bad, as surely if a plane crashed on a runway, ambulances and fire-engines were only minutes away. On the other hand, if anything went wrong over the sea, you were definitely a goner. You would either drown or be eaten for dinner by sharks, and that would be that.

12. The rush of that first take-off still stays with me. The plane taxied to the start of the runway, and there was that delicious pause before the engines revved up to begin the sprint to get airborne. I had a quick crane around to see what other people were doing. I was surprised and a little contemptuous to see many heads buried in newspapers. Surely, I thought, they must be trying to disguise their fear. The cowards! Then I heard the roar of the engines and the race began to get into the sky before the runway disappeared. I was gripped by a silent excitement as I felt the front wheels of the plane lift and bring the sleek metal bird into the heights. My only moment of anxiety came at that moment when immediately after take-off, your stomach feels like it is in your mouth. Once that passed, I felt like I was in heaven, as the land and the houses below were reduced to a patchwork quilt and we were now rumbling across the blue emptiness. How we had gotten there in terms of aerodynamics was still, as it is now, a mystery, not to mention how we were managing to stay airborne, as we were going at what felt to me like only a very steady speed. Still though, the memory of that first childhood flight remains vivid.

MARKS & COMMENTARY

CLARITY OF PURPOSE The writer has a very clear idea of what is needed in a personal essay. The text develops a very good picture of the writer's memories, with excellent imagery adding to his description of his past. **30/30**

COHERENCY OF DELIVERY The essay is well structured and the student maintains the same register throughout. **30/30**

EFFICIENCY OF LANGUAGE USE Apart from a few hiccups, this text shows the writer's mastery of the English language. **28/30**

ACCURACY OF MECHANICS There are few mistakes in both spelling and grammar in this essay, showing an excellent aptitude for the English language. **Marks: 10/10**

Total mark: 98/100 (A1)

SAMPLE ANSWER 3

Write a personal essay on the part that other people's expectations play in our lives.

We all live with other people's expectations of us. Whether they are family, teachers, friends, even practical strangers, we feel some form of pressure to match up to their ideas of who we can be. Positive expectations spur us on, whereas, if they are negative, it can make a person feel unworthy.

practically

they

I have always lived with a form of pressure from my parents and teachers in relation to my future. My two brothers are well on their way to being doctors, while I have no real idea what I wish to do. However, I *do* know I do not wish to have a job cutting people open.

'Then how about dentistry? You can make a wonderful amount of money if you aim to be an orthodontist! Just think about it.' Wise words from my mother. I'll work in a clinic in the city, spending my time looking at mouths ranging from the prepubescent to octogenarian ages. After every patient, I'll look to see when my time is up for the day, only to find there are 5 more hours, and twenty more patients, and it's a Monday. White walls, the smell of disinfectant becoming a part of the oils secreted from my glands, scared little seven-year-olds wetting their trousers in fear. Oh yes, dentistry sounds wonderful. Rated as the most likely to commit suicide, being a dentist might not be the best idea mother.

'Well, aren't you being a tad superior? Is it not good enough for you? Pray, what do you see yourself doing?' She's getting annoyed now, and I can see exactly where the 'conversation' is going, since this is the hundredth time it has occurred:

'I don't know, but I know it isn't dentistry, or medicine.'

'Your brothers are very happy where they are, and if you make a bit more effort, you can get there too. You'll love it.'

'Thanks for telling me how I'll feel.'

'Don't be smart with me young man.'

'Isn't that exactly what you want me to be?'

'Right, if that's how you want to act, you can do the washing-up later, and take Max for a walk. Get some air and sort out that head of yours!'

Of course, the above conversation varies somewhat from time to time. Sometimes I don't have to do the wash-up; I just have to go to my room.

I try to understand where my parents are coming from, but the answer continues to elude me. They already have two children well on their way to being looked up to by *everyone in the world!* So why can't they just call me a black sheep and let me choose a life less ordinary? It seems to be a prerogative of every parent to get their child to a high enough station in order to crow over all the other parents of lesser mortals. Yes, I'm bitter, but that is just because I don't think I can make as much of an impact on society as my darling brothers will. Well, not in the field of medicine or science at any rate.

I have to admit, however, ignoring the expectations of my family has been difficult. Their alternate attempts of either spurring on my abilities, or telling me I wouldn't be able for such and such a life is harrowing to say the least. My father's less-than-subtle attempts at reverse psychology is worth it all however: 'Sure leave him be Mary, the boy barely has the

continued over

continued from previous page

SAMPLE ANSWER 3

brains for bloody ordinary maths in the Intercert (old-speak for the Junior Cert exams – bless), never mind getting all the points for medicine. He'll never do it.' My Dad peeks out at me from under his bushy eyebrows to see if his innovative attempt at motivating me has had its effect. My smirk along with a knowing glance just makes him growl before he repositions the newspaper in front of his face.

To be honest though, I wouldn't want to be an overly sensitive person when coming up against people who think they know what is better for you. There's a good possibility that through this wonderful reverse psychology, one could be brow-beaten into attempting a course not suited to the person, and then, unfortunately, all the 'negative' opinions expressed by your loved ones, become real. 'I really am stupid. I should never have thought I was able for this course.' Quite a dangerous path you tread there Dad. Be warned! Every time something goes wrong in my life, I may take it as a confirmation of all the 'negative' predictions that you made about me. Rather than try to prove you wrong, I may just give up and accept what I have been made to believe is my fate – no job, no partner, no prospects … where does that lead?

Such is the life of a soap character, but I'd say there are teenagers out there feeling a similar form of pressure and self-doubt at the hands of their families. God knows their parents mean well, but there are ways and means to getting the best out of your child.

Therefore, I shall sit on my proverbial stone and theorise how best to deal with my parents, so that we are both happy. I don't believe colluding with their expectations is for my benefit in the long run, as I am sure medicine is not for me. I believe a person needs a certain kind of temperament for such a job, and mine would not be able to handle such pressure. I should relate this to my family. Maybe if I let them know me some more, they will understand my final decision themselves.

MARKS & COMMENTARY

CLARITY OF PURPOSE The essay is quite relevant and focused. The student chooses to concentrate on his personal experience and bring this to bear on the subject of the essay. It could be argued that the student should have made some more general comments about expectations throughout the course of his essay. **27/30**

COHERENCY OF DELIVERY The essay reads nicely and is well-structured. The student adopts a somewhat informal tone and maintains it throughout. The use of his own experience to illustrate the role that other people's expectations play in our lives is quite well managed. **27/30**

EFFICIENCY OF LANGUAGE USE The student displays a good level of vocabulary and varies his sentence patterns. Punctuation is good and the paragraphs well constructed. The student avoids overly-long sentences and makes use of lively and interesting phrasing. **28/30**

ACCURACY OF MECHANICS The students spelling and grammar are of a high standard. **10/10**

Total mark: 92/100 (A1)

SAMPLE ANSWER 4

Write a personal essay on the importance of music and/or songs in your life.

1. Music is an immensely powerful thing, able to create every sort of feeling within your soul; alternately motivating you, or helping you to de-stress. It can convey every emotional peak and rut, along with every shade of grey in between. What can I say? Music is the memoir of my life.

2. My mother used to say that as a baby, I could never go to bed without lullabies playing in the background. The sound soothed me to sleep, giving my mother more time to deal with my older, brash siblings. It is unusual that we humans are so inherently attuned to melody that we can instantly distinguish abrasive tunes from harmony. It is similar to calves being able to walk within moments of being born. It is intrinsic to our being.

3. The earliest song I can remember is 'Yellow Submarine' by the Beatles. It was part of a cassette for children and I used to listen to it all the time when playing in my room. Every time I hear it now, I am transported back to when I was four or five, and I distinctly remember, with crystal clarity, my assiduous attempts to build a tower of Lego. Music seems to be a memory trigger, but who knows why certain events are maintained in our minds and others are not.

4. Songs I heard when I was younger will always hold a special place in my heart – even songs like 'Girls Just Want to Have Fun' by Cindi! I had a wonderful childhood, and any song that reminds me of those times will always take precedence on my list. Such feelings of nostalgia are rarely so powerful than when triggered by music. Even bedtime stories do not have such an effect on me. Indeed, when reading them again, my more experienced brain reads the stories in a different way than before, as I do not have those younger, innocent eyes to look through any longer. But with music, I vividly remember my way of thinking when I was such a young age, and I know that I will never lose that part of myself.

5. When I was nine I began having piano lessons. Suddenly, music other than pop songs entered my life. From simple Chopsticks to Sonata in C by Mozart, I worked my way through each level of piano music. Luckily, my tutor was a benevolent nun who did not force me to do the exams. Therefore, I never felt any stress when playing the compositions or when learning the more difficult pieces. The choice was completely mine when choosing what to play and I learned to challenge myself more and more. A day never went by without my fingers touching the ivory keys of the our piano at home, and even nowadays, I will sit on the stool and lightly play some of the simpler pieces just to regain those feelings of happiness I used to experience. It's strange to think of music as something you'd turn to when you are hurt, distressed, or angry. Usually one would think of going to a friend, but nothing seems to cure my blues like music does.

continued

continued from previous page

SAMPLE ANSWER 4

6. Key moments in my life as an adolescent are few and far between. The first three years of secondary school have completely melded together in my memory and are now pocketed away in the back of my mind, never to be rifled through again. One thing that stands out for me is that I had stopped playing music and did not study it in school. I studied my other subjects. I watched TV. I mused about my various crushes. I slept. It was only in Transition Year that I began to return to life, as they say. I had finally found a group of friends that accepted me for me. I was finally happy and I started to express it. Along with my new friends came introductions to new songs, and it suddenly hit me how much I missed having music in my life. In the following years, music became my study aid. It was the one medium that helped me continue pouring over my Maths book at ten o'clock in the night. 'Float On' by Modest Mouse cheered me up anytime I felt down, and filled me with such happy feelings that even to this day, I like Maths! Lock me up please.

7. I recall one story in a book called Musicophilia by Oliver Sacks. As a neurologist, he was amazed at how the brain sprang into life when music was played near a patient. In one instance, a man was struck by lightening only to become a composer in later life, as the lightning had 'awoken' a musical side to his brain. This is the part where I say, 'don't do this at home kids!' The possibilities with music are seemingly endless. It leads me to believe that humans cannot continue without music in their lives. Even in the direst situations, people will raise their voices and sing about their circumstances. Where do you think the Blues came from? Maybe I can create my own music from my own life experiences. In my short life, I have had many.

8. Death is a fleeting moment in time. It is a moment we will all experience, yet one may only experience a few seconds of 'knowing' before the moment is gone. For the people who are left behind, to carry on without the presence of their loved one, Death is interminable. One more life is gone; the flame has been quenched in their hearts and we must trudge onwards and attempt the uphill slope. If anything, the music at the funeral Mass called out more tears than I could believe existed within my frame. I felt drained of everything by the end of the service. All emotion was gone. All that was left was antipathy. This was the only thing I'd feel within me throughout my struggle uphill. Then the choir struck up one last song, singing quiet harmonies, rising and falling in latent succession. My ear picked out the ascending voice of the lead soprano, and my heart stirred.

9. After this, I learned that music is there for us for the good times and the bad. Music has an inherent quality that makes the listener feel understood, as, in times of need, it can be the most intimate sustenance. The nature of music is in itself sublime. A picture paints a thousand words, while music places you within the picture.

MARKS & COMMENTARY

CLARITY OF PURPOSE The student has written an entirely relevant essay and maintains her focus throughout. **30/30**

COHERENCY OF DELIVERY The essay flows nicely. The student introduces numerous experiences and personal memories to illustrate the role of music in her life. These ideas are well managed. She orders her ideas well, using paragraphs that are focused and sequenced in a coherent fashion. It could be argued that paragraph 8 upsets the flow of the essay, its relevance not becoming apparent until mid-paragraph. The tone is fairly informal, entirely appropriate and is maintained throughout. **28/30**

EFFICIENCY OF LANGUAGE USE An excellent level of vocabulary is displayed, and the student's sentence patterns are varied and never dull and repetitious. Her punctuation is of a high standard, and she uses lively and interesting phrasing, making this a pleasurable reading experience. **30/30**

ACCURACY OF MECHANICS Spelling and grammar are excellent. **10/10**

Total mark: 98/100 (A1)

13 Speeches

Speeches in the Leaving Cert require you to convince your audience that something is the case. For example, you might be asked to convince your audience that celebrity culture has gone too far, or that hope is a sustaining human gift.

PURPOSE AND STRUCTURE

When writing a speech, you will need to use the language of argument, appealing to your audience's intellect through facts, logic and rational argument. You will also have to use the language of persuasion, appealing to your audience's emotions, prejudices and preconceived ideas.

When writing a speech you need to be very aware of the following:

THE PURPOSE OF THE SPEECH

As with all essays, it is vital that you remain highly conscious of what you are trying to do. Remember that you are trying to convince your audience that something is true. As you plan and write your essay, remember that every single paragraph should contribute to this goal. You will be penalised for straying off the point.

FORMAL SALUTATION

When making a speech, it is best to begin with what is known as a 'formal salutation'.

If you are addressing a formal gathering of people, you should begin your speech with the phrase 'Ladies and Gentlemen'.

If there are dignitaries in your audience, you should include them in your salutation; for example, 'Mr President, ladies and gentlemen'.

If you are addressing your classmates, you should open with 'My fellow classmates'.

TONE AND AUDIENCE

Some Leaving Cert questions require you to adopt a serious tone. Others require you to adopt a more light-hearted tone. It is important that you practise writing both serious and light-hearted speeches.

Some Leaving Cert questions don't specify which tone you are to use in your speech. In these instances, you must decide which tone is most appropriate yourself. When doing this, it is important to be conscious of your audience. For example, a speech given to the UN about climate change should have a formal tone. On the other hand, if you are addressing your classmates, you may want to use a more relaxed, light-hearted tone.

Whatever tone you decide to use, make sure you maintain that tone throughout the speech.

WHO YOU ARE

Some speeches require you to imagine you are someone else; for example, you might be asked to imagine that you are a leading politician. It is important to imagine how you would speak as this character, and to maintain the appropriate tone and register throughout your speech.

OPENING PARAGRAPHS

In your speech, you are trying to prove a point. Sometimes, you might want to state this point plainly in your opening paragraph. We see this in the opening of a speech made by the British politician, Stanley Baldwin, in 1932, the year that Hitler came to power. Baldwin feared greatly the possibility of air warfare and the consequences such warfare would have for civilians:

> What the world suffers from – and I have said this before – is a sense of fear, a want of confidence, and it is a fear held instinctively and without knowledge very often. But in my view, and I have slowly and deliberately come to this conclusion, there is no one thing more responsible for that fear, there is no greater cause of that fear than the fear of the air. Up to the time of the last war, civilians were exempt from the worst perils of war. They suffered sometimes from hunger, sometimes from the loss of sons and relatives serving in the Army, but now, in addition, they suffer from the fear, not only of being killed themselves, but, what is perhaps worse for a man, the fear of seeing his wife and children killed from the air.

It is also possible to begin your speech with an 'impact' paragraph that grabs the audience's attention before stating your point clearly in the second paragraph. The 'impact' paragraph might often focus on a shocking statistic, real life story or dramatic event that brings your point vividly to life.

BODY PARAGRAPHS

Each paragraph should focus on a single topic. Each paragraph should support the point you make at the beginning of the speech.

In the body paragraphs of your speech, you can use facts and statistics to appeal to your audience's heads. You can also use real-life stories and emotional language to appeal to their hearts. Every single paragraph should be geared towards one thing: convincing the audience that your point of view is correct.

CLOSING PARAGRAPHS The closing paragraph should briefly summarise the main points of the speech before concluding with a snappy, memorable phrase. It can also be very effective to conclude your speech with a question that will linger in the audience's mind.

SAMPLE ANSWER 1

You have been asked to give a radio presentation on the hopes, fears and dreams of teenagers today. Write the speech that you would give.

Good afternoon listeners. I am here today to talk about the hopes, fears and dreams of the modern teenager.

1. Popular American television series such as the OC and Sweet Sixteen have been dramatizing the lives of teenagers for many years now. Although humorous and entertaining, these programmes also offer us an important insight into the modern teenagers mind and a brief glimpse at their hopes, dreams and fears. Although these programmes only offer us a very generalised view of teenagers, in comparison to my own group of friends, with whom I have spoken extensively about this topic I feel that they reflect many truths. However, as the differences between the male and female mind is so great, I hope to analyse them separately.

This sentence is long and poorly constructed and leaves the reader confused.

2. Many listeners are no doubt familiar with the tale of Cinderella. The hard working young maiden gets transformed into a beautiful lady wearing a flawless ball gown. Well to be perfectly honest the hopes of the average female teenager, as vain and trivial as it may appear, are in the same vein as this tale. This hope is then moulded around the expectations of every teenage girl of the climax of her secondary education – the debutants ball. From first to sixth year this one night on which we are given permission to wear dresses fit for fairytales, is at the centre of every girl's mind. The hopes for the perfect dress, the most eye-catching shoes and, of course, the handsome date are never far from teenagers' minds.

This sentence is muddled, poorly constructed and the student might have been better advised to break it into two sentences.

3. The hopes of a male teenager however are somewhat different while females strive for social acceptance and admiration, men tend to focus their hopes on the sports field. Be it GAA, basketball or soccer the male goal remains the same: to prove his masculinity to those around him. The hope for a county or All-Ireland medal remains to be the primary hopes for my peers. Perhaps this longing stems from that of the original hunter gatherer, who competed with his fellow man, but there is clearly a difference between this and the female outlook.

Once again the student has used a long, poorly constructed sentence that is difficult to read. The student should have used two sentences, placing a full-stop after the word 'different'.

poor grammar

4. Programmes such as Desperate Housewives send out the common misconception that teenage girls dream of living in quiet suburbia with two point one children and a wealthy husband. However, although this may have been a common dream in the late sixties, I feel that modern girls are thinking more along the lines of the comedy Sex in the City. These high powered

independent woman live lives driven by fashion and female superiority, a vision shared by many young girls today. City life encompassed by designer clothes and a party lifestyle certainly seems to fill the dreams of a twenty first century female in her adolescence.

5. While this dream of having the freedom to sit down and chat in a New York coffee shop with your best friends haunts young girls, teenage boys seem to be dreaming of the day when they will be a well paid business executive who drives a new BMW sports car and lives in a sleek apartment comparable to a technological haven. The dream of success is never far from the mind of adolescent boys and is increasingly surfacing in this dog eat dog world. The phrase 'the end justifies the means' unfortunately crops to mind in relation to this longing, as more and more achieving success requires many drastic and questionable actions, all in search for the dream.

The sentence is too long and confusing. The phrase 'crops to mind' is wrong.

6. As clear as it seems to listeners that male and female teenagers think in a very different manner, I would like to draw one comparison between their outlook for the future and their fears. As the end of sixth year draws to a close we look to the future, hoping and dreaming of a prosperous life. However, as I look around the corridors I see sixth years signing yearbooks, browsing through old photos, laughing at stories from our first days in Secondary school. These images that I am confronted with aptly reflect the terror that teenagers face as they are forced to move on. The people who we have learned to love and trust may not be there for us anymore. The fear of change and loss of friends unites men and women who leave the school for the final time and also we anticipate what is still to come. We cannot help but miss what has already passed.

Another long and poorly constructed sentence.

7. Any period of transition in life calls for contemplation. As teenagers develop into young adults they are no doubt faced with food for thought. Hopes, dreams and fears are to the forefront of everyone's minds as we move cautiously on. However, change is imminent and just as the class of two thousand and eight moves forward with one set of expectations the teenagers of the future will look to a completely new outcome. Hopes for the best, dreams for the extraordinary and fears of the unknown will always be prominent in human nature. What form they will take? Only time will tell.

MARKS & COMMENTARY

CLARITY OF PURPOSE

The student has clearly read and understood the essay title. She remains focused on this title throughout the essay, and every paragraph is relevant to the theme.

The student has been asked to write a radio presentation. She fulfils the conventions of a radio presentation, referring to her listeners several times throughout the piece.

To an extent, the student has a clear point of view: boys and girls have different hopes but are united in their fears and uncertainties. However, she would have been better advised to outline this more explicitly and at greater length at the beginning of her presentation. **24/30**

COHERENCY OF DELIVERY

The writer adopts a chatty, informal tone, which she successfully maintains throughout.

The writer makes reasonable use of references and examples, referring to her own experience and popular television programmes. However, perhaps a broader range of examples could have been brought in.

There is a reasonable level of continuity of argument in this essay. Each paragraph focuses on the writer's central theme and more or less logically connects to the paragraph that came before it. The student might, however, have been better advised to state her point of view in a very clear way at the beginning of the essay.

The sequencing of the different paragraphs, whilst not a disaster, could be improved on. Perhaps the references to television programmes could have been kept together. It is also possible that the essay would have read better if the student had grouped the paragraphs on boys together and those on girls together instead of moving back and forth between the two. **18/30**

EFFICIENCY OF LANGUAGE USE

There is a reasonable level of language use in this presentation, with some lively and interesting phrasing, and a variety of paragraph openings and sentence patterns. There is a good standard of punctuation and paragraphing, with each paragraph focusing on a clearly defined topic.

However, the essay is let down by some poor syntax and sentence structures. Many sentences are simply too long, meandering through a variety of clauses and leaving the reader confused. **20/30**

ACCURACY OF MECHANICS

The student displays a good knowledge of spelling and grammar. **8/10**

Total mark: 70/100 (B3)

SAMPLE ANSWER 2

Write a speech in which you discuss the role of sport in today's Ireland.

To the Parents' Association of our town, I wish to speak to you now about the role sport plays in Ireland today. Is it still a method of developing social interaction, or has it just become a commercially viable cash-cow for lucrative investors? As a nation, we must analyse the reasons we play or follow sport, in order to be sure that the role sport plays in our lives is for our own well-being both mentally and physically.

How different is sport today in relation to fifty years ago? In an age devoid of videogames and social-networking sites, children had no choice but to go outdoors and run and play with the other children. Exercise was not termed 'exercise' as it was not looked on as a chore, but rather a release from being stuck indoors. Children happily ran, cycled, and played games, while also eating proper meals. Sweets were a Sunday treat. Altogether, it was a very healthy lifestyle that has been forsaken of late. Outdoor games have given way to computer games and an endless supply of DVDs to watch. Healthy meals have succumbed to fast-foods and an unlimited amount of sweets.

Therefore I believe sport is of the utmost import in Ireland today as it encourages exercise, while being fun for children. And we all know that encouraging sport at an early age is an excellent way to keep children fit, healthy and happy. The benefits in getting children to play sports are numerous:

- Sport develops children's leadership skills;
- It develops organizational, social and team-work skills;
- It encourages children's health and productivity in the classroom;
- It combats physical and mental stress;
- It promotes national pride.

In truth the list could be endless, but what this indicates is easy to see: Sport is very important in progressing a child's way of thinking. As the popular saying goes 'There is no "I" in TEAM'. Learning to work together with other children encourages a healthy view of life as well as heeding to the advice of their parents and teachers in order to learn how to play better. In this day and age, where independence in youth is reaching critical levels – I'm not saying some independence is not healthy, but a child paying no attention to their elders is worrying – learning to listen and being able to take advice from people with more experience is a very good lesson to learn. Luckily, Ireland has many excellent teachers that take time out of their own personal lives in order to encourage this healthy side of children's lives. Children can therefore develop their skills to such a level that, as young adults, they can play for their hometowns and clubs.

continued over

continued from previous page

SAMPLE ANSWER 2

Gaelic football and hurling are still showing themselves to be integral parts of Ireland's national heritage. People throughout the country continue to have intense pride in their representing teams, whether it is because they are connected by familial ties, or are just outright sports fans. An aspect that, in my opinion, has held Gaelic football and hurling high in people's estimations is that it is through the work of volunteers, rather than paid associates, that the game is brought to us throughout the year, every year. The players are like us, working normal jobs to fund their passion for sport. The same goes for every team's hometown club, which are each run professionally by unpaid volunteers. People seem to feel that, as the players are getting no monetary fee when playing for their county, they truly represent the people. This belief increases the sense of Irish pride, which people entering our country can savour as well.

In general terms, sport can still be seen to bring people together. If people just went to work and went home, life would be incredibly dull. However, creating new social spheres is where sport shines. People are brought together sharing a similar love of sport. And Parish clubs come together in competition, which is sometimes fierce. But it is through similar passions and pride that people roar their support for their teams. It is truly an amazing sight.

However, when speaking of sport in a professional sense, I have various concerns on how our children are being conditioned by what they see on TV. Unlike GAA and rugby, where there is a general sense of camaraderie even between the opposing fans, professional soccer seems to boast a culture of segregation. Fans are urged to support their teams in every way they can, monetarily and physically. Soccer has changed from being an enjoyable, passionate game, which encouraged team-playing, to an all-for-what-you-can-get mentality, fostered by the materialistic leanings of business-men. Professional sport is now a business rather than a system propagating healthy social discourse. Players are now competing for positions on a team, not to represent their country or club, but to earn extortionate amounts of money.

Where does all this money come from? Peer-driven young children are being conditioned at an early age to buy the latest soccer shirts of their favourite team in order to appear 'cool' and on top of the latest trends. Business corporations are gorging on the weakness of youth to line their pockets with gold, as well as fund soccer players' gilded lifestyles with an imprudent amount of money for playing games. The lifestyles of these flamboyant soccer celebrities then promote an unhealthy idea of sports. In most senses, this garish way of life should be sorted out by football associations in order to return soccer to the more honourable side of sport *par exemple* Gaelic games. The only good thing about all the hype given to these soccer players, is that it encourages children to emulate them in terms of getting out and playing the game. That is all. Children should be shown by teachers and parents that the lifestyles shown on TV are not indicative of the meaning of sport. Rather, encourage them to find their own meaning by playing the games themselves.

However, one of the few downsides to sports in schools is the fear of being left out of games by students who regard themselves as not being good enough. This fear of exclusion cultivates a dislike of sport in these students and needs to be addressed by attentive teachers and parents. Other downsides would include a lack of facilities in schools, with many schools having to seek help from the local sports clubs in order to have ground available for games. Luckily very few schools are in a situation where it is very difficult to play sports.

But for those people uninterested in sport or physical activity, I cannot urge you enough to get out into the open air and get some exercise. If not for yourself, do it for your children. Combating obesity has become an urgent concern for the state, due to the increasing popularity of 'fast-foods' as well as past-times like video-games and social-networking sites. Not only children, but teenagers and adults are not as active as they once were, choosing to sit at a computer rather than go outside for a walk or involve themselves in anything energetic. This increasing trend is worrying due to the increase in diagnoses of clinically obese people. What we need to do is encourage a love of sports in order for people to see all the good sides to staying fit and healthy.

In conclusion. I feel that sport is as important today as it was in the past. In increasing a sense of social community whilst also keeping people fit and healthy, sport is its own winner. If we can continue to encourage people to play sports rather than staying indoors, the battle against obesity, depression and antipathetic feelings towards others will be a success. I thank you for giving up your time to listen to me and I hope you will encourage your children to partake in more sports.

MARKS & COMMENTARY

CLARITY OF PURPOSE

The student has clearly read and understood the essay title. She remains focused on this title throughout the essay, and every paragraph is relevant to the theme.

It could be argued, however, that her aim is not entirely clear. She seems to get sidetracked by her discussion of the importance of exercise for children, and it is questionable how relevant this is to the role of sport in modern Ireland. **26/30**

COHERENCY OF DELIVERY

The writer makes good use of references and examples. There is a good level of continuity of argument in this essay. Each paragraph focuses on the writer's central theme, and logically connects to the paragraph that came before it. The sequencing of the different paragraphs is sound, though, as mentioned above, she might at times have kept more focused on sport. **26/30**

EFFICIENCY OF LANGUAGE USE

There is a good level of language use in this speech, with some lively and interesting phrasing, and a variety of paragraph openings and sentence patterns. There is a good standard of punctuation and paragraphing, with each paragraph focusing on a clearly defined topic. **28/30**

ACCURACY OF MECHANICS

The student displays a good knowledge of spelling and grammar. **10/10**

Total mark: 90/100 (A1)

SAMPLE ANSWER 3

Write a speech in which you attempt to persuade the audience that the past should not be glorified.

repeats noun / Is this statement backed up later? / took place

1. Ladies and Gentlemen, I am here today to talk to you about the past, and about the way that certain people glorify the past, either out of wilful ignorance or false sentimentality. There are also those people and organisations that, often for sinister motives, attempt to falsely glorify history in order to serve their own ends. All too often, those who eulogise the past tend to forget or ignore the enormous suffering that has been a constant theme of human history. It is all too easy to focus on what went before and view it through the lens of sentimentality and wishful thinking. The picture of the old person who begins a complaint against the behaviour of the current generation with 'In my day' is a standing cliché. People often hark back to the past in reaction to what they perceive to be the faults and vices of the present. We should not start imagining that the human beings who lived before now were free from selfishness and corruption, not to mention pain and suffering.

nobler / awkward phrasing syntax / awkward again / in need of backing statement

2. There is no point in believing that the men and women who came before were of a higher or more noble calibre than today's generation. Although the external props and conditions of human life change, it strikes me as being fair to say that the hopes and aspirations of all peoples everywhere and at all times remain largely unchanged. Most people wish first and foremost for security, food and shelter. After that, we seek comfort in family, friends and loved ones. Some of us then look for more in art, travel and adventure. To imagine that the dreams and hopes of humanity in ages past differed radically from those of the present generation is hugely unlikely given that we all belong to the same species. And equally, we can surely say that the percentage of people who have found happiness and fulfilment in the pursuit of those goals has more than likely remained constant. If anyone thinks that those who lived in an era that was not so dominated by technology and money as this one is were by definition happier or more virtuous than those alive today, they are surely guilty of deluded thinking and a serious lack of realism. It is very easy to romanticise the past; it is far more difficult to see it through an even and unbiased perspective.

syntax / syntax

3. On a darker note, glorification of the past is quite often used for sinister and malevolent purposes. Those who thrive on nationalist and racist prejudices invariably hark back to a time when everything was 'pure' and uncontaminated by those who either come from a different country or have a different colour skin to those who are euphemistically termed natives. The so-called Golden Age, where virtue and purity reined supreme before the introduction of outside forces that led to a degeneration and poisoning of the land and the people, is a common myth that is frequently used as a pretext for violence and ignorant prejudice of all kinds. What typically happens is that the past is viewed in such a distorted and selective manner as to provide a highly simplistic division of 'us' and 'them'. The 'us' are the good guys, representatives of all that is good and true. The 'them' is the group of ignorant, if not downright evil, outsiders who invade or colonise in order to destroy our land and our traditions. By identifying the alien virus, and using the glorified past as a model, we can, through whatever means necessary, create a future that will mirror the past in terms of its goodness and moral virtue.

syntax

4. The most classic example is, of course, that of Hitler and Nazi Germany. As part of the drive to vilify the Jewish people and create a pretext for the most brutal and clinical genocide the world has ever seen, a picture of a mythical Germany that existed before Roman times was created and fostered through the use of a highly selective and historically dubious interpretation of the evidence to hand. As a result of this, the myth that German purity and virtue was at great risk as a result of outside forces, the most

dangerous of which was Judaism, allowed the ground to be laid for the mass-murder that followed. This is only the most obvious example history provides us with. There are many, many more.

5. Let us return to our own day. Although technology and science have many enemies and critics, who quite often point out the deleterious effects of an age dominated by the lab worker and the engineer, it would be both ignorant and irresponsible of us to hark back to an age where some would have believe that our lives were freer and under less impersonal control than they now apparently are. As an example, can anyone deny the advantages brought about by the spread of information technology that dominates the present age? Whereas previously, one was restricted to, for example, waiting weeks, if not months, for the mail service to facilitate communication between family and loved ones who were separated by large stretches of geographical space, we can now, thanks to e-mail and mobile phones communicate more or less instantaneously with anyone in the world if the means are available.

6. The astonishing rise of the Internet has made the world a more open and democratic place than it was even a mere ten or fifteen years ago. Think about how quickly information spreads around the world now as opposed to times past. When our parents were growing up, information on just about anything even slightly out of the ordinary or away from the mainstream of daily concerns had to be sought with energy and determination, requiring at the very least a trip to the local library, if not further afield. Now, thanks to the Internet, most citizens can access a vast database of knowledge and information concerning the world they live in for a very small price. Are we to seriously believe that those who lived in times past were better off as a result of not having that capacity available to them? Although knowledge need not always equate with power, it does at the very least prevent us from falling prey to the worst kind of ignorance and superstition.

7. Likewise, lest we be tempted to exaggerate the so-called freedom and glory of times gone by, let us remember the great improvements in the average standard of living for a typical citizen in the western world. On a daily basis, we completely take for granted the availability of running water that is both warm and clean. Whatever about the failings of the public health service, we know at the very least that if we are in dire need of medical attention we can most often get it. Levels of literacy and learning are at an all-time high and are also taken as a given for the most part. Now immediately I hear some of you cry that I am being highly selective and am choosing to ignore the great poverty and distress suffered in those parts of the planet that remain radically underdeveloped and at the mercy of the forces of tyranny, ignorance and corruption. I would not, of course, deny any of the dreadful suffering that takes place in this day and age. Millions of people across the world suffer from serious malnutrition and disease, and are at the mercy of forces greater than they can control. All I would say is that to think that the fate of these people would have been better had they been born fifty or a hundred years ago is to indulge in highly wishful thinking. And again, thanks to the worldwide revolution in communication technology, we are at the very least made aware of the plight of our fellow human beings and can choose to act in order to improve and remedy the situation. Every day in the media we are told of the situation in those areas most afflicted by famine, war and pestilence. As a result, the possibility of intervention is there. We can no longer hide behind the veil of ignorance that those who lived before us could, with some justification, cite as an excuse for a failure to act.

8. Finally, lest I may sound like I am completely rubbishing the past and foolishly glorifying the present, I should also say that there is of course a great deal to be learnt from what has gone before. On

repetitive sentence pattern

would have us believe

length of sentence

repetitive syntax

punctuation

vocab – word choice

length of sentence

syntax

syntax

continued over

continued from previous page

SAMPLE ANSWER 3

products

repetitive

the most obvious level, we are all the product(s) of the past, whether it be on a personal, collective or national level. The present is only ever the sum of our past experiences, and we are shaped by history in ways that we are often even not consciously aware of. On a more reflective plane, lest some of us are foolish enough to be duped by the notion that everything that has occurred before the very recent present is by definition 'primitive' and 'backward', we clearly need to study the past in order both to learn from our mistakes and to identify our virtues. No area of human life is completely coloured in black or white, it is always differing shades of grey. Proportionately speaking, there were as many noble men and women alive in the past as there are now, as, of course, there were as many selfish and foolish people and ideas then as there are now. We do not need a glorification of the past. Instead we need a clear-eyed, mature and unsentimental view of what has happened before our own time in order to avoid repeating the worst errors of those who brought us to where we are today.

MARKS & COMMENTARY

CLARITY OF PURPOSE The student has clearly read and understood the question. He establishes a clear point of view in the opening paragraph. Each subsequent paragraph serves the aim of arguing for this point of view. However, there is a sense that several of the paragraphs are over-long and drift slightly away from the main point. The student might have been better advised to keep every paragraph focused on the main point of his essay. In general, paragraphs should be no longer than they absolutely need to be. **26/30**

COHERENCY OF DELIVERY The student's argument is set out in a logical fashion. Each paragraph leads neatly on to the next. Each paragraph introduces a topic that is reasonably relevant to the student's central point of view. The student also maintains a consistent tone throughout. However, the student might have been advised to use more concrete examples and specific references. **27/30**

EFFICIENCY OF LANGUAGE USE The student displays a good range of vocabulary, and makes excellent use of the language of persuasion. We see this in a phrase like 'they are surely guilty of deluded thinking' in paragraph 2.

However, the essay is let down somewhat by over-long and confusing sentences, a certain lack of punctuation in some places, and a muddled use of syntax. These failings make the essay unnecessarily difficult to follow at times. The student should have kept his sentences short and punchy. After all, this is a golden rule of essay writing. **22/30**

ACCURACY OF MECHANICS Spelling and grammar are of a high standard. **9/10**

Total mark: 84/100 (B2)

14 Short stories

A short story offers greater freedom, perhaps, than the other genres. However, it requires practise to be able to compose a successful, convincing story. This chapter deals with the components vital to all short stories.

CHARACTER

Characters are probably the most important element in a short story. If your characters aren't convincing and believable, your story won't work. Characters are what people empathise with when they read, and the more human your characters are, the more likely it is that the reader will enjoy what you write. The following are some general tips on how to create convincing characters.

CREATE A CHARACTER PROFILE

The first step in creating a convincing character is to identify what kind of person they are. A lot of the time, students resolve this problem by basing the character on themselves, but a good writer should be capable of creating characters from a variety of different backgrounds.

Some of the questions you need to ask yourself when creating characters are the following:

- Is the character male or female?
- Is the character old or young?
- Are they happy or sad, lonely or indifferent?
- What kind of clothes would you expect them to wear?
- What does the character look like?
- Does the character have any relevant hobbies or interests?

DEVELOP THE CHARACTER'S BACKGROUND

Like real people, characters should have a background. You might not actually include all of the background information in your composition, but it will help you get a better idea of the character if you imagine a background for them. Some relevant questions when it comes to building up a character's background are:

- What does the character do for a living? Do they work or are they in education?
- What's their family situation? Does the character have brothers and sisters? Are his or her parents alive or dead?
- Are they single, in a relationship or married?
- Where is the character from? Is it where the action is set?
- What kind of things does the character own?
- What is the character's relationship to other characters? Will this change over the course of the story?

USE EVOCATIVE LANGUAGE WHEN DESCRIBING THE CHARACTER

One of the most effective ways in which you can conjure up a convincing picture of a character is to use language that precisely and evocatively identifies their personality traits. The possibilities here are literally endless, but the vocabulary list at the end of this chapter (pages 145–9) gives a good starting point for describing characters and their traits.

HOW MANY CHARACTERS SHOULD A STORY HAVE?

Because you have only a short period of time, it is not feasible to develop more than two or three main characters in your essay. Students often go wrong by trying to introduce too many main characters, which they don't have the time or space to develop properly. This can leave the reader confused and dissatisfied. However, it is fine if your essay also features some 'extras' or background characters whose personalities don't need to be developed for the story to work; examples of this would be passers-by or people in a crowd.

SETTING & ATMOSPHERE

Setting and atmosphere are vital to every story. It is important that you describe where the action is taking place. Use descriptive language to create a picture of the setting in the reader's mind and to conjure up its atmosphere.

PICTURE THE SETTING YOURSELF

Use adjectives.

Where appropriate, base the setting of your story on a place you already know.

It is important to remember that it only takes a few words to make a setting seem vivid and atmospheric. For example, 'John walked through the dusty, sun-drenched schoolyard' is much more effective than 'John walked through the schoolyard'.

You shouldn't spend more than a paragraph describing a setting. Remember, you've got a story to tell. Students often go wrong writing hundreds of words describing landscapes at the expense of character and plot.

PLOT

The term 'plot' relates to the events that happen in a story. To put it simply, your story should have a beginning, middle and an end. Before starting to write, it is important to map this out.

PLANNING YOUR PLOT

Determine the situation of your characters at the beginning of your story.

Have a clear idea what will happen to them during the course of the story. Will their lives change? Will they encounter a challenge? Will they meet someone new?

DECIDE HOW THE STORY WILL END

Time and again, students fail to take account of these points, and start to write before they have planned the plot of their story carefully. This leads to essays that meander pointlessly and leave the reader dissatisfied. It also leads to stories that seem to end in the middle because the student has run out of time and has failed to reach a proper conclusion.

Because you only have approximately 1,000 words, every paragraph should be relevant to the plot. For example, it your plot concerns a mugging, don't spend five paragraphs describing what the victim had for breakfast. Get the story up and running from the very beginning of the essay.

N.B. Whatever plot you come up with, make sure it is RELEVANT to the essay title. You can write a story as good as Shakespeare and lose plenty of marks if it is not relevant to the title.

PLAYING WITH TIME

You don't have to begin with the first event of the story and conclude with the final event. When writing narratives, you are always free to play games with how the passage of time is represented, and being able to do so will advertise your understanding of the language of narration.

The following is the opening line of a story that opens with the final event of the story:

As he was led down the corridor to the electric chair, the events of the last few months flashed before his eyes ...

The following is the opening line of a story that begins in the middle of the story:

Jimmy's eyes flicked between the ball going around and around the roulette wheel like a demented mouse and the millions that rested upon the 13 black ...

With this said, do be aware that it is perfectly acceptable to begin at the beginning of the action and end with its ending; indeed, when you are working against time limits – as you will be in the exam – this may even be the most sensible approach.

DIALOGUE

Dialogue is when characters speak to one another. Always be sure to put the character's dialogue in inverted commas. It is important not to include too much dialogue. For the most part, you should only include dialogue that is relevant to the plot. A long, meandering conversation that has nothing to do with the plot will lose you marks. Writing convincing dialogue is real skill and requires a lot of practice. Listen to people around you and read professional authors to see how they use dialogue.

A NOTE ON BEGINNINGS & ENDINGS

The vital thing about your opening is that it makes the reader want to read more. There are many, many ways of doing this.

You could start with a dramatic or exciting event.

You could begin by introducing a character that the reader will instantly find interesting and intriguing.

You could beguile the reader by describing an atmospheric setting. (It is important that you don't spend too long describing the setting before you get down to the business of the plot.)

It is important that your story has a proper ending and doesn't look like you just stopped because you ran out of time. Some stories tie up all the loose ends and provide a very definite resolution. It is also possible to have an ending where the reader is left hanging, uncertain about how events will work out.

Example of a definite resolution:

The sun glinted on the silver trophy as Peter walked up steps, mud on his boots and his sweat-soaked jersey. He looked down on the sea of smiling, cheering faces, one hand on the cup and one hand punching the air in ecstasy. He'd done it.

Example of an unresolved conclusion:

'I'm sorry,' she said, 'I never meant for this to happen,' and reached out to take his hand. In the distance, the traffic began its rush-hour drone and children laughed as they left the schoolyard. He turned away from her with tears in his eyes, and didn't know what to say.

SAMPLE ANSWER 1

'From the moment he woke up, he knew it was going to be a bad day'. Write a short story based on this sentence.

Sean scouted the surrounding landscape for any source of defence. For miles and miles they had been trudging through deep forests where the trees surrounded them, soaring and striving to grasp hold of the clear, cloudless sky. The sunshine was brilliant. The golden light dipped through the leaves on the trees and spilled onto the crunching forests floor.

Sean was amazed by how real this looked, it all seemed too good to be true. He motioned to Alex to go forward. Alex brandished his sword, as Sean was cautious of enemies hiding amongst the trees. He had gotten so far now, that only death could make him turn back.

> This doesn't quite make sense, as it would be impossible to 'turn back' after death

There was a motion. An arrowshot. Noise. Sean paused. This was going to be difficult. If only he could actually communicate with Alex, things would be far easier than they were. But that was impossible. They continued, Sean keeping an eye out in the direction of the arrowshot. An enemy! Sean tensed and sat back as Alex's sword swiped through the enemy, killing him immediately. Satisfied with the kill, and a clear pathway ahead they moved on.

> probably not the best choice of word – 'movement' might have been better

This was their final chance. They continued through the forest until they approached a glittering lake. It shone like a mirror and reflected as one too. There was barely a movement apart from the gentle rippling from apparent light breeze. Once again, Sean was amazed by the real life-like qualities the lake possessed and he longed to swim in the glassy lake and forget about everything. He loved this world. He was free. There was no one to shout at him, no one to hurt him, no one to pressure him, but also no one to love him. It was a lonely life and Sean imagined how his friends would be out in the sun rebelling against the adult world, playing football and doing other strong activities that young boys do. Thinking of this gave him a slight feeling of depression. How can this be happening? What has he done to deserve such torturous and harsh events? Why can't he be at home with his family? Playing outside with his friends? You only live once.

> eventually approaching

> awkward

> 'had' would have been better than 'has'. Also, 'torturous and harsh events' is poor.

Yet here he was a twelve-year-old boy fighting for his life against every imaginable force of evil. Who else goes through this? Not even his friends could see him. He was sure that they would be proud if they could.

There was a crash. Sean checked around to make sure that all pathways were clear and risk free. Once certain, Alex was instructed to continue. How Sean wished to be like Alex. A warrior of the unknown. Built up of strength, honour and loyalty. Brandishing a larger golden sword and shield there weren't actually people like this were there. Sean had often wondered he'll never know. He knew he'd never known. He just had a feeling.

> These sentence fragments ought to have comprised one sentence, broken up with commas.

> Last 3 sentences here are very poor and confusing to read.

A warning was signalled and Sean informed Alex of the impending event. Bullets and arrows were aimlessly shooting towards Alex from all directions. Sean was trying to help in every way possible, sorting through weapons and methods of defence. Although his 'feeling' would not escape from his mind. From the moment he woke up, he knew it was going to be a bad day.

Is it possible for the arrows to be aimless and heading for Alex?

sentence fragment, poorly written

Alex struggled on and defeated the legion of enemies. Relieved, Sean attempted to focus his mind to helping Alex. They were now making their way up a mountain, capped with snow, overlooking the whole kingdom. It was magnificent. The forest below seemed to be hugging the ragged edges of the mountain whose face was being dramatically reflected by the glassy lake.

Sean had never taken notice of the beauties of this world before. Here he was acknowledging the beauty of this second world. He hated himself. He hadn't fought hard enough. He had just let things go. Too much out of hand. He envied Alex's strength and capability, knowing that even if he allows him to die, he will be resurrected and led by someone else, maybe not as unfortunate as Sean.

An army of enemies were silhouetted on the skyline above the mountain. Sean gasped. Determined to win this war, Alex was instructed to proceed and attack. His technique had been so powerful that he almost sliced the air with the precise rapid slaying with his sword. Killing them one by one, Sean's heart lifted. Determination was taking over. He was controlling someone else's life, and was fighting for them as he hadn't for his own. Tears built up and misted his eyes. His view was fogged and he was struggling to continue. He couldn't do it.

awkward sentence

The battle was vicious. Alex truly was an amazing hero. Sean envied him. Although he had only been directing Alex's moves, he felt increasingly weak and faint. It was happening, and he knew it. Unable to control Alex he stopped. Vision blurry Sean rolled back. Alex was killed. This is where he lost all hope.

If he wasn't capable of keeping a computer game character alive, how was he able to keep himself? For months now he's been in this hospital room, only the company of this computer game. Idolising the character of Alex and engrossing in a world so far away from his own helped him to get through his boredom.

engrossed

All day he had the feeling that today was the day. With a final glance at Alex curled on the computerised mountainside, Sean gently slid backwards onto the hospital bed, closing his eyes. It had happened. Game over.

MARKS & COMMENTARY

CLARITY OF PURPOSE

Though a short story offers greater freedom than other genres, when it comes to the purpose, it must be clearly related to the title you have been given. In this case, the student has written a story that is relevant to the title given and he remains focused. The story avoids becoming dreary, and the student manages to keep the reader engrossed by withholding certain key bits of information until the very end, e.g. that the character Sean is actually playing a computer game and is not really a soldier on a battlefield. This device is cleverly used and effective. **30/30**

COHERENCY OF DELIVERY

The student has structured his story relatively well. It starts with Sean and Alex nervously edging towards the battle, climaxes with a battle scene, and ends with the revelation that Sean is in hospital playing a game. Because the student has chosen to withhold information and have the reader believe that Sean is actually fighting a real battle, it is vital that his descriptions of Sean's actions be ambivalent, i.e., when we come to understand that Sean is only controlling a computer character, we need to be able to acknowledge that the descriptions of Sean's actions at the start of the story still remain true. In this regard, the student has managed his story very well.

The story features some sound creative modelling. The student describes the natural environment where the battle is taking place. This is a world that is slightly fantastical, in keeping with the fact that it is a virtual landscape, but the student also manages to make it real and vivid. The character of Sean is well managed. The tone and register are controlled throughout. **27/30**

EFFICIENCY OF LANGUAGE USE

The student displays a reasonable level of vocabulary and varies his sentence patterns, thus preventing the story from becoming dull. His use of short sentences and sentence fragments at times heightens the tension and the drama of the story. However, the student needs to be wary here and not lose control of proper structure. On occasions, his sentences are badly written and a little confusing, e.g. 'Sean had often wondered he'll never know. He knew he'd never known. He just had a feeling'. The story is broken up into logical and well-managed paragraphs, and features some lively and interesting phrasing. His descriptions of the landscape are quite good at times, though they do come close to cliché on occasion, e.g. describing the surface of a lake being like a mirror. The story also contains a number of poorly written sentences. **22/30**

ACCURACY OF MECHANICS

As we have noted before, sometimes in a short story it may be permissible to deviate from the normal rules of spelling, grammar and syntax. The student has no good reason to do so in this story and, in fairness, his spelling and grammar hold up pretty well. **8/10**

Total mark: 87/100 (A2)

SAMPLE ANSWER 2

We will look at how another student handled the same title.

From the moment he woke up he knew it was going to be a bad day.

The sun's heat penetrates exhausted soil and its warmth manifests itself into humid air. Sweet smells of newly cooked pap linger as the new day awakens to African beauty.

All is calm yet ...

Silence roams with the exception of the ibis, a routine alarm for tired eyes.

Nkosi awoke to the blazing rays of the African sun, it is only six-thirty and the temperature is soaring. The Cape Flats shone through his miniature window, the glare off the corrugated iron roofs piercing his eyes. His sisters lay fast asleep so quietly he crept out, bolting the door.

His school was a full two kilometre walk and so he left immediately, forgetting breakfast. He had slept in and couldn't understand why his mother wasn't there.

He set off amongst the worn and usually unattractive township dwellings, shacks made of corrugated iron, old political posters lying astray, aging packing cartons peppered the ground. He felt that something was wrong as he trudged the well worn path through the veldt. The vast outline of Table Mountain soared before him, a silhouette of dusty grey against an ultramarine sky. It was like an old friend to him but in the winter months it grew threatening when the clouds poured over the top, cascading down the sides into the Cape Bowl.

Hunger rampaged his empty stomach but he continued to walk on with little haste, a trail of brown dust kicked up behind him. He reached a small shanty village area called Umzumbe, an area he was always nervous of passing. Usually he avoided it, however today he had little time.

The boys inhabiting this town were violent and drunkards, even at this early hour of the morning. They were always in trouble at school, the teacher taking no mercy. Nkosi felt a surge of fear tyrannize the hunger which roamed his stomach. He turned around a stinking shabine, men lying on benches outside, drenched in alcoholic oblivion. It sickened Nkosi as his father had left the previous year, he left his mother to defend four children on hot African soil, favouring the company of wasted men that he called 'friends'. His dear mother had been abused too many times as a result of his weakness, alcohol, and it was for this reason that Nkosi loathed these men. He tried not to look at them as he walked bravely past, the stench of urine making him cringe. He passed without episode, thankfully, a breath of relief.

Too soon, however, three skellums emerged from behind a shack. Their faces were worn from previous battles, burnt and scarred by the sun of the Cape. They were not much older than Nkosi, yet they towered over him, their clothes bearing the stench of Kaffir beer.

They approached, eyes abundant with menace. They wanted some fun and saw him as a defenceless target for their masculine aggression. Nkosi stopped in his tracks, terrified, wishing he had awoken earlier to abscond this dreadful meeting.

corrugated

he crept out quietly

peppering

'without haste'

but

drunk

They were always in trouble and the teacher showed them no mercy.

Unusual description, not entirely successful.

'abundant' is not appropriate here; 'full' would have been a better choice of word. Sometimes it is best to use the simplest word.

wishing he had woken early and so avoided this unpleasant encounter

continued over

continued from previous page

SAMPLE ANSWER 2

The student needs to pay close attention to her verb tenses. 'Was' would seem to make better sense here

'Referring to him as the 'goody' of the class and saying that he ought to learn a real lesson'

This sentence is poorly constructed.

poorly written

Again a poor sentence, composed of fragments that don't cohere.

investigate

after

This sentence is flawed

Overly long sentence, difficult to follow

unnecessary

forced?

nauseous redundant, 'nauseous' means feeling sick

yet again the student has written a sentence with a number of clauses that don't cohere

unusual choice of word

incapable

He wished his mother had been there – where was she?

His feet gripped the filthy ground beneath him, his palms saturated in sweat, clenching tightly together.

The oldest one taunted him, recalling him as the 'goody' in the class and should learn a real lesson. Grabbing Nkosi by his sachel, soaring above him, the smell of ale and ancient sweat hit Nkosi like a thunderbolt. They each had their turn in a feisty push, an aggressive heave, an abusive thug. The punching only severed, a tear began to roll, no, he had to remain strong, he could not appear weak. Where was his mother?

They yanked his satchel from his scrawny back and began to invade the contents, dismissing them behind their shoulders if they had any educational value. Eventually, proceeding a few more bumps, bashes and bruises the three malicious grins departed, leaving a tormented Nkosi on hot African soil.

He ran to the school, terrified that they were following, but they had no intention of going to school that day.

Running with a pounding heart, his ripped shirt flowing behind him, his bloody eye excruciatingly painful but he knew he had to get away. Reaching the school, a high walled concrete building, he located a bench and sat outside solely to gather his thoughts and breathe mopping the blood from his eye onto his dishevelled shirt, he wepped, sopping endlessly. He only looked up to view two burly black gentlemen, they were police, smartly dressed in their dusty blue uniforms, polished medals reflecting the suns rays and heavy guns holstered at their hips.

He shrank in fear as he realised he could not tell them of his misfortunes, he would no doubt harshly suffer the consequences from his earlier acquaintances.

How did they know what had happened?

He felt terrified that he may be reduced to reveal the names of his attackers, revenge would surely follow. He suddenly felt nautious and incredibly sick, but nothing would come up as he could not recollect his last meal.

Aware of his fear, pain, anxious attitude and fragile condition the officers gently raised him to his feet. It only dawned on him then that one of the officers was his mother's friend, his face occupied a troubled stare, something was wrong. The older officer squeezed his hand and told him that he had news of his mother. The nausiating sensation returned, a gulp of terror eclipsed his throat and closed his throat to air. They announced that she had been seriously injured in an attack the evening before whilst walking home from the local shop. She was recovering in hospital but was going to be fine. It was not as horrific as he had anticipated yet the news weightened his shoulders. His body fatigued, unstable, uncapable of anymore bad news.

The officers escorted Nkosi to visit his wounded mother as she lay dazed in a hospital ward. Holding his mother's hand, squeezing it gently, he comforted her with the notion that all the atrocities of the day would float away by sunrise.

That evening as Nkosi walked home, he watched the purple skyline descend over the Table Mountain, suffocating the African sun. The humid air turned colder, bringing storm clouds which loomed on the distant horizon. A torrential downpour was calling in the distance, it would wash the day away. Nkosi knew however that each passing storm brought pink skies in the early morning and that the hot African sun would deliver a day drenched in new found hope. He contemplated that today was going to be a bad day the moment he woke up.

MARKS & COMMENTARY

The story is relevant to the title and remains focused. The use of an African setting in a Leaving Cert story is uncommon, but makes for an intriguing reading experience and is well managed. However, the story's plot is less engrossing than its setting. **25/30**

The story lacks good narrative shape. Opening well, with a commendable description of the sun's heat and the smells of the morning, the story fails to reach a satisfying climax, and becomes somewhat dull. The story suffers from too much weighty description and the student's efforts to impress with language come at the expense of narrative drive. Though it has a beginning and an end, the main body of the story is poorly managed.

As mentioned above, the student's description of the African setting is well managed. She describes the landscape well, and introduces features and characters to create an effective and plausible world. **24/30**
The student is ambitious in her use of language, sometimes successfully so, but on a number of occasions she uses words and phrases incorrectly and inappropriately. She would seem to have a good vocabulary but, perhaps, needs to put it into greater practice. Her sentence patterns are varied but the sentences are too often flawed, containing a mix of tenses that is awkward to read. She would have been better advised on occasion to use shorter sentences correctly. **21/30**

The student displays a reasonably good knowledge of spelling, though her grammar is occasionally flawed. **7/10**

Total mark: 77/100 (B2)

SAMPLE ANSWER 3

'... after the war ...'
Write a short story suggested by the above phrase.

'What will you do after the war?' I cannot recall how many times I had this question asked of me between 1940 and 1945, nor indeed how many times I asked it of others. You didn't have to be a professional psychologist to realise that the question was posed not just out of curiosity, but also as a psychological trick to help us get through the weeks and months of conflict. By projecting forward to a faraway time free of guns, blood and the prospect of a violent death that awaited us once the war was over, we found it that bit easier to cope with the trials and torments of what was lying before us in the immediate future.

Sitting on the grass outside a huge aircraft hangar in the south of England, I reflected that I didn't have to be where I was. I was Irish and had chosen to volunteer to fight against Hitler out of my own free will. I can't say that I did so out of any particularly high-minded ideals. Instead it seemed just too good a chance of escaping the dreariness of life in Ireland in the 1940s. The prospect of a bit of excitement was also too enticing to pass up. I remember the suspicious look the recruiting officer with an enormous moustache in Belfast gave me when he asked why I wanted to fight for Britain, when my own government had declined the generous offer of Churchill to come in with him in the fight against Hitler. I couldn't think of any deep motivation, so with the wisdom of my eighteen years I just blurted out that 'it was all a big adventure which I did not want to miss'. The moustache twitched a little, before I caught the words 'silly little fool' being muttered under a breath as the officer began to fill out the necessary papers.

That had been four years ago. I had been home on leave three times since then, and had been looked upon with a mixture of suspicion and wonderment by the neighbours and the locals. In the pub in the evenings, I would do my best to keep entertained those who wanted me to tell them stories of adventure and excitement in return for a pint. A lot of the time I had to embellish my tales for, as someone said, war is a matter of long periods of boredom punctuated by sudden bursts of excitement. Often people would ask me what I would do after the war, as surely after such excitement I could hardly go back to a quiet farming community where the most exciting thing that ever happened was the visit of a small fun fair every summer. I told them that I'd try to get through the war first without worrying about what would happen after.

On my last visit home, my mother had begged me tearfully not to go back. It was August of '44 and she had read of the massive casualties suffered by the paratroopers in the Normandy landings. Was it not enough, she said, that my father had died only eight years previously? Was I to make her into a grieving mother, as well? I did my best to calm her fears, but it was almost impossible. She screamed at me as I left the house that God's curse would be on me in hell if I made her the only woman in the village to have lost a son in the second war. I roared back that, with the help of her prayers, I would do my best not to, and was glad when two days later I returned to barracks in England.

On a balmy September morning a week afterwards, I was preparing for battle once again. Our mission was to drop on a small Dutch town called Arnhem, which neither I nor any of the other lads had heard of, and capture and hold the bridge in the middle of it that ran over the Rhine. Within two days, so we were told, our tanks and infantry would arrive to relieve us. The enemy would be outflanked, a big push into Germany would follow, Berlin would be reached in no time, and then we could all really start worrying about what to do after the war.

We were pretty confident as we hung around waiting to get going. Some lads smoked cigarettes one after the other, savouring each one in the fear that it could be their last. Others kicked a football around, while some just stood by themselves, contemplating what lay ahead. We were all pretty relieved when the order came to board the plane. I spent most of the hour long flight dozing. Images of home and my mother flitted through my mind as I went in and out of sleep. I had absolutely no intention of being the only war casualty of the village.

Just under an hour into the flight I was jolted into full consciousness by the sound of flak breaking around our aircraft. We stood and waited for the door to open and for the green light to come on that would signal us to jump. Thirty seconds later I was floating through the Dutch skies above a wide expanse of flatland. The air was filled with parachutes and it was easy enough to feel confident with such a weight of numbers. We had been told to expect very little opposition.

I had no sooner hit the ground and disentangled myself of my parachute then I heard a cry of 'Germans!' About two hundred yards to the right ran a road along which three half-tracks full of the enemy were speeding. I opened up with my Bren gun, and watched as the grey helmets disappeared beneath the sides of the vehicles. The halftracks sped on toward Arnhem, obviously intending to garrison the only worthwhile target in the area: the bridge. Whoever had told us this was going to be a Sunday stroll obviously had no idea what they were talking about.

On the march toward our objective, I was with the units bringing up the rear. As we neared the town, we were constantly under attack by small groups of the enemy, who would let the main force go by and then attack the stragglers in order to break up the column bit by bit. As the group I was with approached a crossroads about a half-mile from the bridge, we came under serious fire from the upper stories of a hotel. Each of us bolted for cover. I ran across the road in a mad dash to get behind a large car I thought would give me good protection. As I did so, I felt a sharp jolt in my left shoulder and dropped my gun before throwing myself behind the car.

As I lay there with German bullets striking the car like an angry hailstorm, I noticed my thigh was soaking wet. Was my mother's prophecy going to come true, and would I die in the streets of this Dutch town on a Sunday in September? I looked down to realise that a bullet had struck my sidepack and exploded the cans of condensed milk inside. I felt sheepish for a moment, before the throbbing pain in my shoulder made me forget my embarrassment.

I lay there for a few hours until our lot had cleared the area and I was brought back to the rear for proper attention. I felt as if my arm was barely hanging on to my body. The doctor who treated me told me that the bullets had sliced right through my tendons and that I would surely be out of action for three to four months, if not longer. The news brought conflicting emotions. The guilty part of me felt glad to be getting a ticket out of the war, for the short-term at least. The more noble part hated the thought of leaving my friends and comrades-in-arms to fight on while I rested safely back in England.

I was lucky in the end. I was put on a flight back across the Channel with one of the returning planes, lucky to escape the fiasco that was about to engulf my division at Arnhem. Back in London, I was told that the damage to my shoulder was so severe that I would be extremely unlikely to be in a fit enough condition to jump from a plane for at least ten months. Eight months later the war was over.

So it came about that on a sunny day in July of 1945 I was on a bus heading home to my sleepy village, having been discharged and thanked for my efforts. I had no idea what I would do now that the big adventure was over. The transition to peacetime felt like it was going to be a difficult one. I was only twenty-three. As the bus pulled away, I paused to look at the sleepy square of the village. Nothing much seemed to have changed since I had left. I threw my bag over my shoulder and climbed the hill toward home. After the war had begun.

MARKS & COMMENTARY

CLARITY OF PURPOSE This is an excellent example of short-story writing. The story is entirely relevant to the title given. Well written, with plenty of style and freshness, there is an anticipatory rise to a very satisfactory climax. **30/30**

COHERENCY OF DELIVERY The writer shows a keen interest in, and knowledge of, the events during World War II. The atmosphere of urgency is well created in the events just prior to the climax. The student has structured the story well. He effectively introduces minor characters, such as the recruitment officer. **30/30**

EFFICIENCY OF LANGUAGE USE The student shows an exceptional ability with the English language. His sentences are well written. He uses a variety of sentence patterns and avoids being dull. What is most impressive is the way he structures and controls some of the longer sentences. The language is emotive in many places, helping the reader to empathise with the main character, his comrades, and his mother. **30/30**

ACCURACY OF MECHANICS Perfect spelling and grammar. **10/10**

Total mark: 100/100 (A1)

VOCABULARY TO LEARN

VOCABULARY FOR NEGATIVE PERSONALITY TRAITS

Mendacious	someone who tells lies all the time
Avaricious	someone who is greedy and grasping
Contemptuous	someone who scorns everything
Lascivious	someone who is interested only in sex
Slothful	someone who is lazy
Gluttonous	someone who overeats
Atavistic	someone whose personality is primitive
Oafish	someone who is brutish and stupid
Boorish	someone who is graceless and uncivilised
Sadistic	someone who enjoys inflicting pain
Pusillanimous	someone showing a lack of courage or determination
Combative	someone who enjoys conflict or argument
Homicidal	someone inclined towards murder
Hideous	someone who is frighteningly ugly
Deviant	someone who strays from the norm
Cretinous	someone who is extremely stupid
Troglodyte	someone deliberately ignorant or old-fashioned
Moribund	someone who is on the verge of dying
Ineffectual	someone who is incapable of making a difference
Fiery	someone likely to fly off the handle
Temperamental	someone who is very moody
Incompetent	someone incapable of doing their job
Rancorous	someone of a spiteful disposition
Cantankerous	someone bad-tempered, usually old
Monotonous	someone who is very boring
Devious	someone cunning and deceitful
Saturnine	someone with a gloomy outlook
Taciturn	someone who is cold and distant
Reticent	someone who holds something back, usually in speech
Morose	someone with a miserable outlook
Truculent	someone who is hostile and bad-tempered
Dismissive	someone who rejects things in an arrogant way

VOCABULARY FOR POSITIVE PERSONALITY TRAITS

Buoyant	someone with an optimistic outlook
Sanguine	someone with a cheery personality
Iconoclastic	someone who goes against the status quo
Effervescent	someone with a very bubbly personality
Inclusive	someone who includes everybody
Impartial	someone who is extremely fair
Penetrating	someone who sees things in an insightful way
Diplomatic	someone who is good at negotiating
Steadfast	someone loyal and reliable
Refined	someone with very good taste
Modest	someone who doesn't boast about their achievements
Jovial	someone who is very jolly
Affable	someone friendly and easygoing
Singular	someone who is one of a kind
Exuberant	someone enthusiastic and energetic
Engaging	someone who makes good company
Valiant	someone who is very brave
Upright	someone who acts morally
Virtuous	someone who always does what is right
Empathetic	someone who is sensitive to other people's feelings
Charitable	someone who helps other people
Pious	someone who is very religious
Magnanimous	someone who is charitable in victory
Munificent	someone who is very generous
Candid	someone who is very honest
Punctual	someone who is always on time
Indefatigable	someone who never gets tired or gives up
Dogged	someone who is very persistent
Rigorous	someone who is very exact and accurate
Tenacious	someone who sticks to their purpose
Indomitable	someone who cannot be defeated

VERB VOCABULARY FOR SHORT STORIES

The final aspect of short-story writing we will explore is the issue of verb vocabulary. Verbs are often thought of as words that describe actions (for example, to run, to hit, to wake). However, some verbs deal with states (for example. to be, to sleep, to exist). A good knowledge of verbs is vital for every type of composition, and it can prove especially valuable when it comes to writing a short story. In the short story, more than any other genre, you will be rewarded for showing your creativity. Displaying a good knowledge of verbs is an excellent way to make your writing colourful, and to let your creativity shine through. There is nothing duller than a short story where the same two or three verbs are used over and over again. So use a variety of verbs whilst making sure you know what each one means and that you are using it appropriately.

In view of the importance of verb vocabulary for story writing, the lists beginning below (pages 147–9) include some of the more common *verb classes*. In essence, a verb class is a group of verbs that all relate to performing an action of a particular type. Consequently, if you are describing any given type of action in a short story, it may be useful to identify what class this action belongs to, and to see if there are any verbs in the categories below that you can usefully use.

VERBS OF MOTION

To stroll	To pace	To scuttle	To trot	To mince
To canter	To gallop	To pick	To crawl	To travel
To creep	To stride	To march	To skip	To hop
To waltz	To strut	To amble	To fly	To motor
To drive	To pilot	To sail	To skipper	To cycle
To zip	To ride	To steer	To navigate	To control

VERBS OF TRANSFER AND TAKE

To give	To present	To award	To receive	To deliver
To endow	To exchange	To reward	To offer	To accept
To grab	To seize	To annex	To arrogate	To grasp
To nab	To expropriate	To appropriate	To apprehend	To steal

VERBS OF SPEECH AND ARTICULATION

To say	To announce	To declaim	To pronounce	To preach
To assert	To orate	To whisper	To proclaim	To denounce
To argue	To suggest	To claim	To shout	To scream
To articulate	To convey	To whimper	To imply	To hint
To insinuate	To accuse	To interrupt	To relate	To narrate
To tell	To outline	To delineate	To converse	To outline
To verbalise	To exclaim	To utter	To mutter	To communicate

VERBS OF BEING

To persist	To endure	To exist	To subsist	To last
To be	To remain	To persevere		

VERBS OF PERCEPTION AND CONSUMPTION

To hear	To see	To taste	To smell	To feel
To intuit	To listen	To observe	To sniff	To touch
To scrutinise	To note	To register	To absorb	To experience
To watch	To enjoy	To imbibe	To consume	To eat
To drink	To gorge	To snaffle	To pick	To smoke
To inhale	To slam	To skull	To wolf	To bolt
To choke	To cram	To stuff	To spy	

VERBS OF INTIMACY

To hold	To embrace	To cuddle	To stroke	To kiss
To caress				

VERBS OF THOUGHT

To cognise	To think	To evaluate	To judge	To balance
To cogitate	To solve	To resolve	To analyse	To critique
To argue	To propound	To prove	To speculate	To engage
To dwell	To reflect	To consider	To intuit	To philosophise
To theorise	To conceive	To study	To examine	To imagine
To fantasise	To daydream	To ponder	To meditate	To contemplate
To deduce	To reason			

VERBS OF DESIRE, LIKE AND DISLIKE

To want	To need	To desire	To long for	To hanker after
To crave	To covet	To loathe	To despise	To hate
To abhor	To detest			

VERBS OF PERMISSION AND PUNISHMENT

To allow	To facilitate	To permit	To condone	To encourage
To sanction	To proscribe	To prohibit	To taboo	To forbid
To disallow	To punish	To penalise	To levy	To fine
To sentence	To impose	To chastise	To discipline	To rebuke
To castigate				

VERBS OF WORK

To labour	To create	To slave	To exert	To toil
To drudge	To graft	To build	To erect	To engender
To earn				

VERBS OF ENCOURAGEMENT AND DISCOURAGEMENT

To praise	To exhort	To encourage	To hearten	To cheer
To support	To daunt	To dampen	To put off	To discourage
To depress	To dissuade	To dismay	To dispirit	To disincentivise

15 Punctuation

By separating and grouping words together in different ways, punctuation performs an essential role in helping the reader understand what they are reading. Consequently, if you want your written work to effectively communicate its message, it is vitally important to master at least the basics of punctuation.

, THE COMMA

The purpose of the comma is to divide the words of a sentence into groups that are in some way related in terms of meaning or action.

WORDS OR PHRASES IN SERIES Always use a comma to distinguish between the items in a list, except where one of the items (usually the last one) is preceded by 'and.'

EXAMPLES

The farmer kept cows, sheep, horses [no comma] and pigs.

Jimmy is interested in sport, music, film [no comma] and literature.

The First World War saw the emergence of trench warfare, the invention of new weapons, the introduction of conscription [no comma] and a militarisation of civilian life.

ADJECTIVE USE When you are using two or more adjectives to describe the same noun, use a comma to distinguish between these adjectives.

EXAMPLES

The novel is written in a clear, engaging style.

She was a bright, attractive girl.

It was a dark, stormy night when the robbery occurred.

SETTING OFF COMMENTS AND PHRASES Commas are used when you introduce an extra phrase into a sentence. This phrase will usually comment on the sentence or introduce new information. Place a comma before and after the phrase.

EXAMPLES

Dublin, the capital of Ireland, is a very busy city.

Oranges, for example, are a rich source of vitamin C.

The Leaving Cert, after all, is only an exam.

There is, of course, no cure for the common cold.

Paddy Murphy, the previous chairman, was re-elected.

Comedians and clowns, who spend much of their time making others laugh, often suffer from depression.

AFTER A LONG INTRODUCTORY PHRASE If you start a sentence with a long introduction, set this introduction off from the rest of the sentence with a comma.

EXAMPLES

After holding out for two weeks, the kidnapper finally surrendered.

Although Vincent van Gogh scarcely sold a single painting while alive, the fame he achieved after his death has ensured that only millionaires can now afford his work.

SETTING OFF CONTRASTING OR ALTERNATIVE PHRASES When a sentence contains two phrases that contrast in meaning, divide these phrases using a comma.

EXAMPLES

The criminal did not deserve the death penalty, however horrific his crimes may have been.

It is people, and not guns, who are responsible for murder.

Enthusiasm, not aggression, is the key to succeeding in sport.

: THE COLON

Though using the colon (:) is quite straightforward, students invariably make a mess of it by confusing the colon with the semi-colon (;). Basically, the colon has two purposes: to introduce a list or quotation and to preface an explanatory phrase or clause.

INTRODUCING A LIST When listing a number of items, use a colon to set off the listed items from the rest of the sentence.

EXAMPLES

Meningitis has three symptoms: skin rash, nausea and muscle stiffness.

When making a speech it is important to be aware of three things: the audience, the venue and the purpose of the speech.

The Beatles consisted of four members: John, Paul, George and Ringo.

INTRODUCING A QUOTATION The colon is used to divide the quoted text from the introductory text. Do recognise, however, that this is only done when the quoted text is independent of the structure of the introductory sentence; when it is integrated with the meaning of the main sentence, don't use a colon

EXAMPLES

Yeats describes this situation well in 'Sailing to Byzantium': 'That is no country for old men'.

In *Hamlet*, Gertrude instructs her son to stop his unseemly grieving: 'Good Hamlet, cast thy nightly colour off.'

The words on the packet make the message quite clear: 'Smoking causes lung cancer.'

In the following example, the quotation is embedded in the main sentence so no colon is used:
When Yeats suggests that [no colon] 'that is no country for old men', he might well be describing the scandalous state of nursing homes in Ireland.

INTRODUCING AN EXPLANATION A colon is used when the first part of a sentence introduces an idea or event that the second part explains.

EXAMPLES

This is easily the worst day of my life: I've lost a libel case, and I now owe damages and costs to the plaintiff.

We would hear a great deal less about UFOs and lake monsters if people obeyed one of the basic principles of reasoning: the simplest explanation is usually the correct one.

The method for success is the same in every sport: concentrate on your own performance, not your opponent's.

; THE SEMI-COLON

We use a semi-colon to join independent clauses or sentences together.

INDEPENDENT CLAUSES An 'independent clause,' is part of a sentence that will stand as a separate sentence in its own right. For example: 'It was the worst of times; it was the best of times'. The two phrases 'it was the worst of times' and 'it was the best of times' are independent clauses, because each of them make a complete sentence.

SUBORDINATE CLAUSES A clause that cannot stand on its own as a separate sentence is known as a subordinate clause. Take the following example: 'Like a conventional pet, a snake needs to be looked after properly.' The clause 'a snake needs to be looked after properly' is an independent clause because it will stand on its own as a separate sentence. However, the clause 'like a conventional pet' is a subordinate clause because it cannot stand on its own as a separate sentence.

EXAMPLES

He was in bad shape; he had two broken arms and a fractured rib.

His only aim was to pass the exam; his percentage was unimportant to him.

She decided to walk to work; it was a nice day and she needed the exercise.

He often donated blood these days; he knew how important it was.

COMMAS AND SEMI-COLONS Use a comma to distinguish between an independent and a subordinate clause. Use a semi-colon to distinguish between two independent clauses.

If you are a little confused as to where a comma or a semi-colon can be used, try breaking the sentence into smaller sentences. If you create two proper sentences by doing this, use a semi-colon. If you can only get one, use a comma.

’ THE APOSTROPHE

INDICATING POSSESSION

One of the most common uses of the apostrophe is to indicate when a particular item belongs to a person or a person-like entity. It is also used to indicate that something is part of something else.

The possessive of a singular noun: When indicating that something belongs to *only one* person or thing, add an apostrophe and an *s*.

EXAMPLES

The bird’s plumage   The boiler’s element   A goalkeeper’s glove

THE POSSESSIVE OF A PLURAL NOUN

When indicating that something belongs to several persons or things, put the apostrophe after the *s*.

EXAMPLES

The parents’ council   The animals’ sanctuary   The plumbers’ union

The possessive of nouns that are already plural: To indicate possession for nouns that are made plural, add an apostrophe and an *s*.

EXAMPLES

The men’s room [‘men’ is already plural]   The women’s association

The children’s class   The media’s role

The possessive of nouns in series: If one thing belongs to a group of people, add a single apostrophe and an *s* to the last named person in the list of owners. If each person in a group has separate ownership of an item, put an apostrophe and an *s* after each person’s name.

EXAMPLES

Collective ownership	*Singular ownership*
John, Tommy and Fred’s band	Scott’s and Zelda’s hearts
Crick and Watson’s theory	John’s, Bill’s and Martina’s coats
Laurel and Hardy’s films	

THE POSSESSIVE OF NOUNS ENDING IN S

When a noun ends in *s*, you have two options: either add an apostrophe followed by another *s* or simply just add an apostrophe. Whichever you do, however, be sure to do so consistently; don’t use both rules in the same essay.

EXAMPLES

Keats’s poetry OR Keats’ poetry

Steve Davis’s droll humour OR Steve Davis’ droll humour

WHEN NOT TO USE AN APOSTROPHE The most common mistake in terms of apostrophe use is using the apostrophe to indicate when a noun is plural. In particular, try to avoid the following errors.

EXAMPLES

Incorrect	*Correct*
The music of the 1990's	**The music of the 1990s**
I bought three CD's	**I bought three CDs**
Two student's graduated	**Two students graduated**

INDICATING OMISSION The second major use of the apostrophe is to indicate when a letter or group of letters are left out in a word. As a general rule, omission is indicated by putting an apostrophe in the place of the missing letter or group of letters.

EXAMPLES

I shouldn't go [the apostrophe is put in instead of the *o*]

She didn't do it	**You'll never understand**
They're running late	**It's a long way to Tipperary**

IT'S AND ITS By far the most common mistake people make when using the apostrophe is confusing *it's* for *its*. The rule for distinguishing between the two is simple:

EXAMPLES

It's = short for 'it is'

Its = possessive case of 'it' [i.e. something belonging to *it*]

Admittedly, this is rather confusing, but there's nothing for it but to learn the difference.

EXAMPLES

It's a cold day outside.

The comet disintegrated on its journey around the sun.

It's very cold because its thermostat is still broken.

It's that time of year again when it's painful to go shopping.

- THE HYPHEN

As a way of making two words operate as one, the hyphen (-) plays a major role in tightening up expression.

Use a hyphen when the words *better, best, ill, lower, little* or *well* are used to describe a verb that is immediately followed by a noun:

EXAMPLES

His best-known work

The better-prepared player

The ill-informed politician

The lower-priced tickets

The well-dressed announcer

Use a hyphen when making a compound term from a noun and a verb ending in *ing* or *ed*:

EXAMPLES

The alcohol-fuelled car

Her hate-motivated resilience

Use a hyphen when making a compound term from a number and a noun:

EXAMPLES

thirteenth-floor apartment

nineteenth-century history

Use hyphens to join coequal nouns:

EXAMPLES

writer-critic

soldier-athlete

warrior-prince